ASK
SUZE®

. . . ABOUT STOCKS AND BONDS

ALSO BY SUZE ORMAN

You've Earned It, Don't Lose It
Suze Orman's Financial Guidebook
The 9 Steps to Financial Freedom
The Courage to Be Rich
The Road to Wealth
The Laws of Money, The Lessons of Life
The Money Book for the Young, Fabulous & Broke
Women & Money

Riverhead Books
a member of
Penguin Group (USA) Inc.
New York
2007

ASK SUZE®

◆

...ABOUT STOCKS AND BONDS

SUZE ORMAN

This publication is designed to provide accurate and authoritative information in regard to the subject matter covered. It is published with the understanding that the publisher and author are not engaged in rendering legal, accounting, or other professional services. If legal advice or other professional advice, including financial, is required, the services of a competent professional person should be sought.

While the author has made every effort to provide accurate telephone numbers and Internet addresses at the time of publication, neither the publisher nor the author assumes any responsibility for errors, or for changes that occur after publication.

Ask Suze® is a federally registered mark owned by Suze Orman.

People First, Then Money, Then Things™ is a trademark owned by Suze Orman.

Certified Financial Planner® is a federally registered mark owned by the Certified Financial Planner Board of Standards, Inc.

The term Realtor® is a collective membership mark owned by the National Association of Realtors® and refers to a real estate agent who is a member thereof.

RIVERHEAD BOOKS
a member of
Penguin Group (USA) Inc.
375 Hudson Street
New York, NY 10014

ISBN 978-1-59448-969-3

Printed in the United States of America
1 3 5 7 9 10 8 6 4 2

Book design by Deborah Kerner and Claire Vaccaro

THE BIG LEAP

Many, many Americans lost money in the stock market from 2003 to 2004—and many of us who *didn't* lose money of our own have read frightening stories about others who did. The result is that many of us are now permanently gun-shy about investing in stocks. How can we know the proper time to buy and sell, we wonder, and how can we be sure that the companies we invest in are on the up-and-up?

Well, there are no guarantees in the stock market, and if you are a person who lies awake at night worrying about whether every penny is safe and sound, then stocks may not be the best investment for you. But that doesn't mean you shouldn't invest. For most of us, with a long time line—at least ten years until we need the money we're investing—stocks still offer by far the best potential for the growth of our money. I believe that you really *can* learn to invest in stocks and other investment vehicles yourself, and that if you learn and follow the few simple rules contained in this book, you can do so with a reasonable degree of safety. In the long run you may do better than many an expert would do for you.

Remember, you will never achieve a sense of power over your life until you have power over your money. And that means taking control of how your money grows.

This book presents questions and answers that, taken together, will tell you much of what you need to know to begin investing in stocks. Hopefully, in time many of you will feel knowledgeable and confident enough to chart your own financial course. Others may be more comfortable working with a financial adviser. There are many excellent ones out there, and you should feel free to seek their help. Ultimately, however, it is your money and your responsibility. So if you choose to work with a professional, remain an active participant. See him or her as a partner, not as a surrogate investor.

It has never been easier—or, believe it or not, safer—to invest your money in stocks. If you have a computer in your home, the information available to you on the World Wide Web is extensive, generally accurate, and at your fingertips 24 hours a day. I urge you to explore the financial resources on the Web: the most instructive sites, the newsletters of stock trackers and economists, company annual reports, and much more. On my own website, *www.suzeorman.com,* you will find links to just about every major financial site. And if you don't own a computer, you have many other options. If you have cable TV, you can easily flip to the financial news channels or watch *The Suze Orman Show* on CNBC. And scores of new business books find their way into bookstores and libraries every year.

For now, the financial classroom is right here in your hand. With the aid of these questions and answers, you will gain a solid foundation for a basic, satisfying, and potentially very rewarding investing life.

A BRIEF ECONOMICS LESSON

Interest rates, economic growth, unemployment, inflation—these are terms we hear every day. While most of us have a rough working knowledge of their meanings, we'd be hard-pressed to explain the impact they have on our daily lives. But they do have an impact—especially if we are invested in the stock market. So before we get into the heart of this chapter on stocks, let's take a moment to walk through some basic principles of economics.

We'll begin with *interest rates*. Interest rates are an indication of how much it costs to borrow money. When interest rates are high, people are slower to borrow to buy big-ticket items, such as houses or cars. When interest rates are low, consumers are quicker to take on debt, because paying it off will be less expensive. And when people are out there spending money, the economy grows.

As the economy grows, jobs are created, which means unemployment goes down. When there are fewer people out of work, employers generally have to look harder for workers and pay them more. Sounds like a good thing, doesn't it? Not necessarily, because low unemployment and rising wages are factors that contribute to *inflation*. In a period of inflation, goods and services cost more, and money doesn't buy as much. Inflation occurs at times of high employment because as more people make more money, prices go up. (This is partially because companies' costs go up when they have to pay higher wages, and partially because when people have more money, they want to buy more than the economy is able to produce, which triggers that most basic economic principle: the law of supply and demand.)

A side effect of inflation is an increase in interest rates. The government tends to raise interest rates when the economy shows signs of inflation, in order to slow people's buying and curb economic growth. But higher interest rates also make it more expensive for companies to raise capital by borrowing, and that cuts into their profitability—which is one of the chief things investors consider in valuing stocks. Also, when interest rates are high, yields go up on bonds, and bonds begin to look like better investments than stocks. So investors take money out of stocks and put them into bonds, and stock prices fall. So inflation, as you can see, is an enemy of the stock market.

It's fascinating, isn't it? What seems to be good for you as a worker—lots of jobs and higher wages—may be bad for you as an investor. And the inverse is also true. The markets tend to go up in reaction to "bad" economic news, like a moderate increase in unemployment or a slowdown in wage growth. (Note, however, that I said "moderate." If unemployment is high, growth stagnant, and consumer spending low, that's just as bad for stocks as high interest rates are.)

The long bull (up) market at the end of the 20th century was truly unprecedented. It can be attributed to an economy that was in a remarkable state of balance. Economic growth was steady, but for a long time not too fast; unemployment was low, but wage inflation stayed reasonable; and interest rates declined more or less gradually as price inflation subsided. But history indicates that bull markets are followed by bear (down) markets—which are in turn followed by bull markets. That's why it's wisest to go into the stock market knowing that you're in it for the long haul. It's best not to get too excited by short-term upswings and not to despair when the market dips.

With this in mind, let's take a closer look at some of the terms used to describe the economy and how it's measured.

What is the difference between a bear market and a bull market?

If you are an investor, a bull market can give you many happy days—and a bear market can cause you many sleepless nights. A bear market usually means that over a prolonged period of time the market has declined by at least 20 percent. A bull market means just the opposite—that over a prolonged period of time the market has gone up by at least 20 percent.

What is the consumer price index?

The consumer price index (CPI) measures changes in the prices of everyday consumer goods, such as housing, electricity, transportation, and clothing. The CPI is commonly known as the cost-of-living index. Financial analysts keep a close watch on the CPI, since any upturns can be signs of inflation.

What is the index of leading economic indicators?

This index is perhaps the most closely watched index of them all. It is made up of approximately a dozen different reports, such as stock prices and employment information—including, for example, how many claims for unemployment were made across the country in a given recent period.

Many analysts and economists believe that this index can essentially predict the future of the economy—thus the name "leading economic indicators."

What do people mean when they talk about the gross domestic product?

The gross domestic product (GDP) is the estimated total value of services and goods produced by corporations in this country. This is a hugely important measure, since it tells analysts and economists whether our country's economy is growing at a healthy rate.

What is the durable goods report?

The durable goods report is another important indicator. It tells analysts about goods such as TVs, ovens, refrigerators, and cars. If no one is buying these things, the economy tends to slow down.

What is the producer price index (PPI)?

The producer price index is actually a family of indexes that measures the average change over time in the prices domestic producers of goods and services receive for their wares. PPIs measure price changes from the perspective of the seller. This contrasts with other measures, such as the consumer price index (CPI), that measure price change from the consumer's point of view. Sellers' and consumers' prices may differ due to government subsidies, sales and excise taxes, and distribution costs.

More than 10,000 PPIs for individual products and groups of products are released each month. PPIs are available for the products of virtually every industry in the mining and manufacturing sectors of the U.S. economy. New PPIs are gradually being introduced for the products of the transportation, utilities, trade, finance, and service sectors of the economy.

How are PPIs used?

Producer price index figures are widely used by the business community as well as by the government. They are often used as an economic indicator, since PPIs capture price movements before goods and services hit the retail level. Therefore, PPIs may foreshadow later price changes for businesses and consumers. The president, Congress, and the Federal Reserve employ these figures in formulating fiscal and monetary policies.

How does the producer price index differ from the consumer price index?

While both the PPI and CPI measure price change over time

for a fixed set of goods and services, they differ in two critical areas: (1) the composition of the set of goods and services included, and (2) the types of prices collected for the included goods and services.

The target set of goods and services included in the PPIs is the entire marketed output of U.S. producers. Imports are excluded. The target set of items included in the CPI is the set of goods and services purchased for consumption by urban U.S. households. This set includes imports.

The price collected for an item included in the PPIs is the revenue received by its producer. Sales and excise taxes are not included in the price because they do not represent revenue for the producer. The price collected for an item included in the CPI is a consumer's out-of-pocket expenditure to purchase the item. Sales and excise taxes are included in that price because they are part of what the consumer pays to purchase the item.

What exactly is the Fed, and why is it so important?

The "Fed" is short for the Federal Reserve Bank, this country's central bank, with headquarters in Washington, D.C. The Fed not only oversees all the banks in this country, it also has the power to dictate the rate of interest it charges smaller banks to borrow from it. Most banks borrow from the Fed at a so-called discount rate, and the Fed charges them interest. Another interest rate that the Fed influences is called the federal funds rate.

What is the federal funds rate?

The federal funds rate is the interest rate one bank charges another, when one bank lends another money.

What is the prime rate?

The prime rate is the interest rate banks charge their most significant customers. By significant, I'm talking about giant corporations and big businesses. This rate doesn't affect the ordinary investor, you are probably thinking, but think again. If you want to borrow money from a bank or other institution, the interest rate you will be charged is based on the going prime rate, plus a few percentage points. If IBM wanted to borrow money from a bank, it would be charged the prime rate. If you wanted to borrow money from the same bank— say, to finance a new house or a car—you would be charged the prime rate plus.

STOCK BASICS

I hear a lot of talk about stocks, but I must admit I'm not even sure what a stock is.

When people talk about stocks, they are usually talking about common stocks. A common stock is a certificate that represents partial ownership in a corporation, whether it's a big national corporation like General Electric or a little corporation out in Minnesota that makes corkscrews. When you buy a share of a stock, you are effectively buying a part of that corporation, and therefore you have equity (i.e., you are part owner) in it. Stocks are securities are also known as equity investments.

What are the advantages of investing in stocks?

Three advantages: growth, growth, and growth—provided you pick the right stocks. Compared with other investment vehicles such as CDs, bonds, gold, real estate, and Treasuries, stocks have provided investors with the best annual investment returns. To give you an example, over a period of nearly 80 years, from 1926 through 2005, the average return of the stock market as a whole was 10.4 percent a year. Over time, the stock market truly does provide the best opportunity for your money to grow.

I've always thought that the stock market seemed like legalized gambling. Is it really a safe way to invest my money?

Safe is a relative term: How much safety do you need? Or, putting it another way, how much risk can you tolerate? Historically, you should know that there has hardly ever been a ten-year period in which stocks have not outperformed every other single investment you could have made. Period. Granted, history does not always repeat itself, but this is a pretty spectacular indicator. The ten-year period is crucial, however. If you don't have at least ten years to let your money remain invested, you could be taking a significant risk, depending on what is happening in the overall economy.

What if an emergency arises and I have to get my money out of my stocks? Can I do so easily?

Yes. You're asking about something called liquidity, and most American and many foreign stocks are highly liquid, meaning that you can easily sell them. In most cases, you can turn your shares of common stock into money in three business days. But that doesn't mean that you'll be able to sell them at a profit or even for as much as you paid for them; that depends on which stocks you own and when you need to sell.

Tell me about the disadvantages of investing in stocks.

Nothing is certain in the stock market. Just because stocks, in my opinion, are the best investment vehicle for the growth of your money over time does not mean that you will make huge profits—or any profits at all, for that matter—*in any given period of time.*

The stock market seems so complicated! Can I invest in it on my own?

Yes, you can. The stock market *is* a complicated entity that many people have spent much of their lives studying. One reason it is complicated is that it is made up of people just like you and me, buying and selling, and no one will ever be able to figure out exactly why we buy and sell when we do. In general, however, the stock market is absolutely something you can learn enough about to make safe and wise investment decisions. You will need to be patient, you will need to know how to gather information, and you will need to know yourself pretty well so that you do not buy or sell on impulse or hang on to a stock long after you should have sold it because you love it. But all these things have been learned by millions of people.

Why does the price of a stock go up or down?

Supply and demand. Demand for a particular stock by investors such as you and me pushes the price of the stock up. If there is less demand for a stock, or if people who own it want to sell it at any price, the stock's price will go down.

What determines demand for a stock?

You do, you and millions of other investors. At bottom, the price of a stock is controlled by your perceptions, more or less well informed, of the company's future prospects. I'll talk more later about the many factors that go into the making of those perceptions. But the rule is pretty obvious: If the informed word is that this stock is going nowhere fast, then demand for the stock will fall and so will its price. (Also, when many investors unload their shares, increasing the supply, the stock's price can fall further.) If the company's earnings are better than anticipated, or an important financial analyst recommends that investors buy the stock, or the company has a new product that the public loves, or if a new and well-regarded CEO comes on board, demand for a stock will go up and so will the stock's price. There are often other factors involved, as I said, but this is essentially how demand works.

TYPES OF STOCK

What are income stocks?

Income stocks are stocks of stable companies that generally do not reinvest a big part of their profits back into the company each year. This means that those profits can be distributed to the shareholders in the form of dividends. If you want income via dividends and capital appreciation, these are the stocks to invest in. Many stocks raise or lower their dividends yearly, so your income can change.

What are growth stocks?

Growth stocks are typically stocks of companies whose primary objective is to grow. The dividend income from such a stock is usually small or nonexistent, since many of these companies are just starting out and/or plowing most of their earnings back into the company. In my opinion, investing in good-quality growth stocks is one of the very best ways to make a satisfactory investment return over the long haul; remember, the long-term average annual growth rate is more than 10 percent. People who buy growth stocks do so because they believe the company in which they own shares will increase its profits over the years, and that the growth in profits will be reflected in the stock price.

What are value stocks?

Value stocks are typically stocks that have gone down in price but remain a good buy. Value stocks are measured in relation to their company's underlying assets—cash, real estate, plants, and equipment, for example—more than in relation to its earnings potential. People buy a value stock solely based not on future growth of the company but on the fact that they are getting shares of a solid company at a good price and that in time the market will realize this. When this happens, up goes the stock's price.

What are speculative stocks?

Speculative stocks don't have much of a track record. They are the riskiest stocks out there, which means they can make you—or lose you—the most money. You have to ask yourself if the risk is worth it. Typically, speculative stocks are issued by companies that are brand new or that few established investors have heard of. Many of the new Internet stocks fall into this category—a good name for them might be speculation.com.

What are cyclical stocks?

Cyclical stocks are stocks of companies that are closely aligned with what is happening in the business cycle—that is, with whether the economy is in a growth phase or is slowing down. These stocks can include steel companies and original equipment manufacturers (OEMs) of such items as automobile chassis or airplane parts. If you trade in cyclical stocks, you must be fairly sophisticated financially, and you also have to keep your eyes open for the economic indicators. If the economy is growing at a decent clip and production is keeping pace with increased demand, the earnings and stock prices of cyclical stocks will probably rise. If the economy isn't doing so well and consumers are turning their backs on new cars, for example, the earnings and stock prices of these companies will likely fall.

What are small-cap, mid-cap, and large-cap stocks?

Everything with a "cap" in it refers to a company's market capitalization, meaning the total amount of capital the company has at its disposal from all the shares investors have bought. This in turn signifies its size. (Companies of different sizes have historically demonstrated different returns.) Although different financial institutions define these categories differently, the following are what the designations mean:

- *Small-cap.* Small-cap funds invest in companies with market values of under $2 billion (80 percent of the top 5,000 publicly held companies—as well as companies not ranked in the top 5,000). Small-cap funds are subject to greater volatility than those in other asset categories.
- *Mid-cap.* Domestic mid-cap funds invest in companies with market values of $2 billion to $10 billion (about 15 percent of the top 5,000).
- *Large-cap.* Generally, large-cap companies have a market value (capitalization) of over $10 billion. They are typically well established, with solid histories of growth and dividend payments.

What are blue-chip stocks?

Blue-chip stocks are the biggest of the large-cap stocks. They are what we usually think of as the heavy hitters: Exxon, Merck, and Microsoft, for example. All blue-chip stocks are large-cap stocks, but not all large-cap stocks are blue-chip. Blue-chip stocks have enormous liquidity, earnings, staying power, and economic importance.

What are American Depository Receipts?
American Depository Receipts (ADRs) are stand-ins for shares of non-U.S. corporations that are primarily traded on non-U.S. exchanges. It is very hard for most investors to buy those stocks directly. ADRs make it possible because they are traded on the U.S. exchanges.

What is the difference between common and preferred stock?
Common stock is the class of stock that most people buy and own. But a company can also issue what is known as preferred stock. Like shares of common stock, shares of preferred stock represent partial ownership of a corporation. The difference is that if you own preferred stock, you have a legal "prior" claim on the company's earnings, including dividend payments. This means that in times of trouble you will be paid your dividend before the owners of common stock participate in any dividend or gain. Also, your dividend is fixed, unlike dividends on common stocks, which can vary. And if the company goes bankrupt, as an owner of preferred stock you will share in the company's remaining assets, if any, before the owners of common stock do. People usually buy preferred stock because they want income, and preferred stocks generally pay not only a fixed but a higher dividend than common stocks. The downside is that preferred stocks very seldom benefit from growth in the company—again, because the dividend is fixed. They perform similarly to bonds, and are considered a debt of obligation of the company. But unlike bonds, preferred stocks do not have a maturity date. People buy preferred stock because they like the fixed dividend and they know that they have first dibs on the money in case of a default.

What are convertible preferred stocks?
Convertible preferred stocks are shares of stock that start out

as a preferred stock but can be changed into common stock. Because of this conversion feature, the price of convertible preferred stock reacts more to the growth of the company than does the price of straight preferred stock.

If I own preferred stock that issues me a dividend, is that dividend tax-free?

Many preferred stocks do not qualify because they are actually making an interest payment, not a dividend payout. And interest payments don't qualify for the great tax break. So be very, very careful.

INITIAL PUBLIC OFFERINGS (IPOs)

Recently I wanted to buy shares in a company in my hometown, but the company spokesman says they are not publicly traded. What does that mean?

Many companies do not trade publicly, which means that they are privately owned and the public cannot buy shares in them. These companies are known as privately held corporations. Typically, they are owned by a single family or by a consortium of investors, neither of which is obliged by law to declare to anybody (except the IRS) how much money the company is making year to year.

Why would a company want to go public?

Because it wants to raise money. It aims to grow bigger and better, and in order to expand and prosper, it requires or simply wants the capital that comes from offering shares for sale in the public market. If I owned a pharmaceutical firm, say, and I needed to raise a lot of money to fund research for a new drug that promises to cure baldness, I would offer shares of the ownership of my company—common stock—to the general public. This is known as going public. This money would come into my pharmaceutical firm through an initial public offering (IPO).

How does a company go public?

A company going public uses a lead underwriter, or a brokerage firm that takes the company to the public markets via a stock offering.

What are the "primary" and "secondary" markets I sometimes read about in connection with IPOs?

They are, respectively, the original buyers and the later buyers of the stock. When shares of a company are initially offered, they are sold in what is called the primary market at a specific price. Let's say my company has contracted with a particular brokerage firm to take my stock public. The brokerage offers all the shares that are being sold at a set price: $15 a share. This is the primary market for those shares. The opportunity to buy a stock in the primary market for the IPO price is usually reserved for the brokerage firm's best clients. The people who buy shares in the primary market then have the right to turn around and start selling those shares to the general public in the open market. This is the secondary market, or aftermarket. There, the price fluctuates. Most of us get to purchase securities or stocks in the secondary market.

THE MARKETS

How many stock markets are there in the United States?

There are many, many different stock markets in the United States, but the ones that you will hear most about are the New York Stock Exchange (NYSE), the American Stock Exchange (AMEX, or sometimes ASE), and the NASDAQ. Think of them as arenas, or forums, in which people and companies can trade securities. Let's look at them one by one.

What is the New York Stock Exchange?

The New York Stock Exchange, or NYSE, traces its history back to the Buttonwood Agreement of 1792—a pact between brokers and Wall Street merchants that spelled out how they would barter securities. It is still located on Wall Street in New York City, and is the largest and best-known stock exchange in this country, as well as the one with the tightest requirements for companies to become listed and traded. A company will not make the grade with the NYSE unless it is financially strong and an industry leader. In exchange for the privilege of being listed on the NYSE, a company must pay an annual fee.

Brokerage companies, incidentally, describe themselves as members of the New York Stock Exchange. This means they have bought a "seat" on the Exchange, which in turn means that one of their employees carries out orders to buy or sell stock on the floor of the exchange. It is expensive to become a member of the NYSE, usually costing a one-time payment of well over $1 million.

What is the American Stock Exchange?

Like the NYSE, the American Stock Exchange is a central auction market. This means it conducts business on a trading floor, where traders buy and sell securities from specialists, or market makers, in a specific stock. Established more than a century ago, it moved to its present Manhattan location in 1921. The AMEX is known as a major exchange for options (more about these later) as well as stocks. Although the AMEX merged with the National Association of Securities Dealers (NASD) in 1998, the exchange still operates separately.

What is the NASDAQ?

The National Association of Securities Dealers Automated Quotations, or NASDAQ, is the youngest of these three markets. Although the NASDAQ lists stocks from just about every industry, it is best known for its listings of technology companies, including Cisco Systems and Intel. It is the second-largest stock market in the United States. Launched in 1971, the NASDAQ is the nation's first over-the-counter, or electronic, stock market, linking buyers and sellers via a computer network. Brokers and dealers make a market in individual stocks by maintaining an inventory in their own accounts. They buy or sell when they receive orders from investors. Start-up companies issuing stock in initial public offerings frequently list on the NASDAQ.

Buying or Selling a Stock

What do you think the markets are going to do in the future?

In order to tell you what I think about the future of the stock market, I first have to go back and tell you a little bit about the past of the stock market. In 1966 the Dow Jones Industrial Average was 874, and in 1982, 16 years later, it was 875. This is not a typo; the market was just one point higher in 1982, but in between there was plenty of up-and-down movement. During those 16 years we were in what was known as a secular long-term down market. Within every secular bear market there are what are known as short bull market cycles—maybe a few months, or a few years—where stocks regain 25 percent or so of their losses. Then they'll turn right around and head down again.

From 1982 to 2000 we entered what was known as a secular bull market, where the market went from 875 to approximately 11,700. However, within those 18 years the market experienced secular bear trends such as in 1987, when the market when down 22.6 percent in just one day.

In the year 2000 we started another secular bear market, which should last until approximately the year 2015, but please remember that in every secular bear marker there are bull market cycles. And that is what I expect to happen to us right now. We will have periods when the market is up 10 percent, 20 percent, even 30 percent; it could happen in a six-month period or three years. Then it will go back down. We are in for a period of up and down, up and down. That is why it is very important that you watch your portfolios very, very carefully. Now, all of this is very fine and well if history repeats itself, but that, my friends, is a big *if* because anything can happen to upset the historical action of the market, such as a terrorist attack or corporate scandals yet to be uncovered. So the above will only hold true if nothing unexpected happens.

Why do I always hear you say you need at least ten years or longer if you are going to invest in the stock market?

At the end of 2002, the NASDAQ index, which controls many of the big-name technology stocks, had declined approximately 74 percent from its high of 1999 and the first half of the year 2000. That tumble caused many investors to lose 50 percent or more in their retirement plans, stock portfolios, and mutual fund investments. And you need to understand that to recoup a 74 percent loss takes a 275 percent increase. Amazing, but unfortunately true. So even if the markets were to go up 9 percent every single year, it would take just over 15 years just to break even. That's why I think it is so important to understand that stock investing only makes sense when you have a 10- or 20-year time frame; sometimes you will need all the time to make up for losses.

What do you mean by "all or nothing" investors?

What I have noticed is that people either invest all of their money at once or they invest nothing. Or they sell all of their stock at once or they keep it all. They either do everything or nothing. And this can be very dangerous. There is nothing wrong, if something goes wrong, in selling 20 percent. And if something continues to go wrong, you sell another 20 percent. Unfortunately, many of you hold on until your investment becomes worthless and it's too late to do anything.

When I buy stock in a company on the stock exchange, how is my ownership recorded?

Traditionally, by certificate, though today most of us never see certificates of the companies we buy stock in. We see our stock purchases noted on monthly brokerage firm statements, and we receive transaction slips that say we purchased them. When the stock we bought is kept at the brokerage firm through which we purchased it, the brokerage firm is said to be holding our stocks for us in street name, or as a book entry.

Can I get my stock certificates if I want them?

Absolutely. If you want your stock certificates, you can request them, and they will be sent to you. Incidentally, most people guard these certificates very carefully, usually locking them away in a safe-deposit box at their bank.

In your opinion, which is better—to take delivery of the stock certificates or to leave your stocks in street name?

I prefer to leave my stocks in street name with my brokerage firm for the following reasons. First of all, ease. If I want to sell stock, all I have to do is make a phone call or place a trade online, and my wishes are carried out. If I hold my own certificates, I have to physically transport them to the brokerage firm to be sold. Second, timing. Let's say you want to sell your shares quickly when you're on a business trip. If your certificates are in a vault somewhere, you won't be able to. Third, a reputable brokerage firm sends you a monthly statement and arranges for your dividends to be paid immediately into your account. These services keep you abreast of the market for your stock and save you time.

I've often seen TV shots of Wall Street in action, with all these people jumping up and down, screaming, waving bits of paper. What are they doing, for heaven's sake, and what does it have to do with my stock orders?

It has everything to do with your trading orders, and the next time you visit New York, I recommend that you go and see what actually happens at 11 Wall Street, because it is quite a spectacle. Let's say you place an order with your stockbroker (who can be anywhere in the world these days), telling him to buy 200 shares of IBM stock. The broker receives your order, then sends it, via computer, to the order department of his firm, which relays it, again via computer, to a clerk on the floor of the New York Stock Exchange, where IBM is traded. The clerk passes your order on to the floor trader who represents your brokerage firm. The floor trader, armed with your "buy" order, tries to find another floor trader who, for whatever reason, wants to sell those 200 shares of IBM. (The jumping up and down, etc., usually occurs on unusually good—or bad—days.) The two traders haggle for a moment, settle on a price, and execute the order. All this information is then reported back to your broker, who lets you know what price you ended up paying for your 200 shares of IBM. A couple of days later, you will receive confirmation of your trade.

What if no one on the NYSE wants to sell the stock I'm trying to buy?

On the New York Stock Exchange, you will always find a seller, and you will always find a buyer for the stock you want to sell. You just might not get the price you want! Every stock on this exchange has what is known as a specialist, or a market maker. If no one else wants to buy your stock, the specialist has to. This way, there is always a market in the stock you want to sell on the NYSE.

How do I place an order to buy or sell stock?

You do it by placing a "market order" with your broker. But to do that you need to know a little of the terminology. Bear with me: This is the language of the market.

What is a market order?

A market order is an instruction to your broker to buy or sell your stock at the best price the trader can get for you at a particular time. Let's imagine that you are trying to buy 500 shares of the Orman Corporation. The day before, the Orman Corporation closed at $27 a share—that was the last trade price. When you enter your market order with your broker, you are contracted to buy 500 shares at the best available price. Does this mean you will pay $27 a share for your 500 shares of the Orman Corporation? Not necessarily. The actual price you will pay might be higher or lower, depending on the current bid price when your order makes its way down to the trading floor, what the seller is asking for the stock (the ask price), and what is happening to that stock and in the market generally. Share prices sometimes change quickly.

What are bids and ask prices?

A bid is the highest price any prospective buyer of a stock is willing to pay for a share of that stock at a particular time. An ask price is the lowest price acceptable to a seller of a stock. The bid and the ask prices together are a quotation. The difference between them is known as the spread. Bid and ask prices are the two numbers that the person who is taking your order to buy or sell stock will throw at you. He or she will say, for example, that your stock is trading at $27 bid and $27.25 ask. If you want to buy that stock right now, the best price on the floor is $27.25, so if you place a market order that is probably how much you will pay. If you want to sell your stock, the bid—the most someone is willing to pay—is $27 a share, so if you place a market order you might get only that amount. When you know the bid and the ask prices you can use that information to decide at what price you might be willing to buy or sell a stock. Remember, with a market order there are no price guarantees. But you *can* set the price at which you are willing to buy or sell your stock. This is known as a limit order.

What is a limit order?

A limit order is an order to buy or sell a specific number of shares of stock, with one very important condition: You will buy or sell only if you can get the exact price that you want or a better price on those shares. In other words, you are limiting the amount of money you will pay to buy that stock or the amount you will accept to sell it. Say you are still trying to buy those shares of the Orman Corporation. In our earlier example, they were trading for $27 a share. But you don't want to pay that much. You call up your broker and tell him or her that you want to enter a limit order of $26. That means the broker's trader may buy shares only if and when the price reaches $26 or lower. Similarly, when you enter a limit order to sell Orman shares at $27, that means that you will accept only a price of $27 or above.

What is a stop loss order?

A stop loss order is a protective mechanism, used to lock in a profit or to keep you (hopefully) from losing more than a predetermined amount of money on a stock. It is an instruction to your broker to sell your stock once it has traded at a specified price known as the stop price.

This is how a stop loss order works. Imagine that three years ago you bought stock in the Orman Corporation at $9 a share, and now it is trading at $27. You've done pretty well! Indications are that the price of the Orman Corporation is going to continue to go up, but your instinct is to protect that nice profit that you've built up over the past three years. You don't want to sell the stock if it's going to keep rising, but you also don't want to see it go back down to $9 a share and watch your profits go out the window. Here is where a stop loss order comes in handy. You enter a stop loss order at $24 a share. If the price of the Orman Corporation begins to fall and drops down to $24, your stop loss order immediately becomes a market order, and you will get the best price a trader can sell your stock for at that moment. Remember, a stop loss order means that when your stock hits a particular price you want to sell. It does not say at what price you will actually sell the stock. For this, you need a stop sell limit order.

What is a stop sell limit order?

A stop sell limit order is an order that declares that you want to sell your stock at a specific price or not at all. So if the Orman Corporation is at $27 and you want to protect your profits, you could place a stop sell limit order of $24 a share. This means that if the stock goes to $24 you want to sell it, but only if you can get exactly $24 a share. The problem with this kind of order is that you may not get your price, and if you don't, then you may not sell your stock at all. Just because Orman Corporation stock traded at $24 a share does not mean that it was your shares that sold at that price. If the stock price is plummeting fast and goes past your stop sell limit order, you could still be holding the Orman Corporation when it falls to $23, $18, or even $16 a share. This is why many people prefer to use a stop loss order. With a stop loss order, you will sell no matter what, for as soon as the stock hits your stop price (or goes lower than that price), your stock will be sold for the best price the trader can get. Hopefully, that price will be close to your stop price.

When I place an order to buy or sell stock, how long is it good for? Do I need to keep renewing it?

There are many ways to enter an order. The two that you will most likely be dealing with are known as a good-till-canceled order and a day order.

A good-till-canceled order, or GTC, states that you are willing to buy or sell a certain number of shares of stock when they reach a specific price. As the name suggests, the order will remain in effect until the stock reaches that price—in theory, whether that's next week, next year, or seven years from now. If the stock does not reach that price, then your trade simply won't take place. With a GTC order, you have to monitor the stock carefully, because if you change your mind and no longer want your order to be executed, you have to make sure that you cancel the order. Many brokerage firms actually do have a set amount of time for which they will let you keep a

GTC order in effect without your having to renew it. If your firm doesn't have such a policy, watch out—you may end up buying or selling a stock when you no longer want to.

A *day order* is used only with limit orders, and is good only for the day that you place the order. If the stock does not hit your designated price on that day, and you still want to buy or sell it, you can place another order of any kind the next day.

Does the brokerage firm care how many shares of a particular stock I buy?

Years ago it did, but not now. Shares of stock are traded in what is known as round lots and odd lots. A *round-lot order* is an order to buy or sell 100 shares, or multiples of 100. If you were going to buy 500 shares, that would be five round lots. An *odd-lot order,* on the other hand, is an order for fewer than 100 shares, or for a number of shares that is not a multiple of 100.

BUYING ON MARGIN

What does it mean to buy stocks on margin?

Buying on margin essentially means that you are buying stocks with borrowed money. When you buy stocks outright—say, 100 shares at $50 a share—you fork over $5,000 in cash. That's it. Buying on margin is different. Suppose you want to buy those same 100 shares of that stock, but you don't have $5,000, or don't want to spend it right now. If you qualify, your brokerage firm will lend you up to half the $5,000. So all you have to do is hand over the remaining $2,500. You have just purchased stocks on margin.

What is the minimum amount of stocks or money one can have in a margin account?

About $2,000, but each brokerage firm sets its own minimum amount.

Why would the brokerage firm want to lend me money?

You know the answer to that one! The firm isn't going to lend you that money for free. You're going to pay interest. This interest is another source of income for the firm. Not only that, but they are going to hold the stock you purchase as collateral against this loan—so they have nothing to lose and everything to gain.

Why do people buy stocks on margin, even though it costs them to do so?

Think about it. You can control up to twice the number of shares that you actually have the money to buy. Many people think of buying on margin as taking out a mortgage on their stocks. They do it with the hope that their stock will go up in price and make them twice the amount of money they would have made if they had bought half as many shares with cash. As long as their additional profit exceeds the interest they have to pay to the brokerage firm, they are sitting pretty. Most day traders buy on margin.

What is the danger of buying on margin?

The danger for you, the investor, is huge. It comes into play when the stock you bought on margin goes down in price. By law, the brokerage firm cannot let the stock price fall below a certain percentage (usually 30 percent) of what it has lent you. If the stock does go below that, the firm issues what is known as a margin call, whereupon you could be in trouble.

Why? What is a margin call?

A margin call means that you, the investor, must come up

with the amount of money needed to bring the brokerage firm's risk down to the required level. If you do not have the money to do this, the brokerage firm will sell your stock and take its money back. (Even if you do have the money, your margin agreement with the stockbroker may allow a sale of these shares or other shares you own without your permission.) If there is any money left, the brokerage firm will return it to you. With any investment, there is a tradeoff between risk and reward. Buying on margin can increase your reward, but it also seriously increases your risk. I personally would advise you to stay as far away from margins as possible, unless you consider yourself a sophisticated investor and are willing to take a big financial loss in pursuit of a possible greater return.

SECURITIES PROTECTION INSURANCE

What happens if the brokerage firm that holds my stocks goes under?

There is something that will protect your investments, up to a point, in the event that your brokerage firm goes belly-up. The Securities Investor Protection Corporation (SIPC) is a non-profit membership corporation established by Congress in 1970 that insures cash and securities in customer accounts for up to $500,000 (including up to $100,000 in cash) in the event that your brokerage firm files for bankruptcy. If your brokerage firm is a member of the National Association of Securities Dealers (NASD)—and you should deal only with a brokerage firm that belongs to the NASD—then you will be covered by the SIPC.

What happens if I have three accounts at one firm? Does that $500,000 SIPC ceiling represent a total for all three of my accounts, or for each one separately?

The $500,000 is the amount of insurance offered for each and every account that you hold in a separate capacity, i.e., as a custodian, a joint tenant, or a sole owner. But if you are a customer who, in a single capacity, maintains several different accounts held with the same investment firm or brokerage, then you would be considered a single customer as far as the $500,000 ceiling is concerned.

I have more than $500,000 in an account. Does this mean my money is at risk?

Most major brokerage firms do carry additional private insurance above and beyond the $500,000 provided by SIPC. There are some brokerage firms that will cover you for any amount that you have in your account, and others that set a cap on the extra coverage they carry. So please make sure that you ask your firm to verify the amount and who provides the coverage. This is also one of the reasons why it is so important for you to establish that your firm is a reputable one, with significant protection behind it. But remember, the account insurance offered by the SIPC and any other insurance coverage your brokerage firm has in place does not protect against losses due to market fluctuations. Note, too, that no insurance will protect against securities that aren't registered with the Securities and Exchange Commission.

THE INDEXES

I keep hearing about stock market indexes. What are these?

All stock market indexes are indicators used to measure and report changes of value in representative groups of stocks. An index is simply a statistical indicator of how a particular group of stocks (or bonds) is performing. There are several key indexes that track changing values in the stock and bond markets. The most familiar stock index is the Dow Jones Industrial Average, which is an index based on 30 large-cap stocks. If these 30 stocks happen to go up in value overall, so does the Dow Jones index.

What is the Dow Jones Industrial Average?

The Dow Jones Industrial Average (DJIA) is by far the most widely known, widely quoted daily financial index in the world. But as an indicator of the overall stock market, it is also somewhat misleading, since it tracks only 30 large-cap blue-chip companies and because it's "price-weighted," which means that the highest-priced securities in the index exert a disproportionate influence on how the DJIA does in general.

What are the 30 stocks that the Dow Jones is made up of?

As of January 2007:

3M Company
Alcoa
Altria Group (formerly Philip Morris)

American Express
American International Group
AT&T
Boeing
Caterpillar
Citigroup
Coca-Cola
DuPont (E. I.) de Nemours
Exxon
General Electric
General Motors
Hewlett-Packard
Home Depot
Honeywell
Intel
International Business Machines
International Paper
Johnson & Johnson
J. P. Morgan Chase
McDonald's
Merck
Microsoft
Procter & Gamble
United Technologies
Verizon Communications
Wal-Mart Stores
Walt Disney Co.

The Dow Jones is made up of stocks that supposedly represent areas of public interest. Microsoft and Intel were the first two technology stocks to be added to the Dow, in 1999. Also added in 1999 were SBC Communications and Home Depot, while companies like Chevron, Sears, Union Carbide, and Goodyear Tire were taken off.

Is there more than one Dow Jones average?

Yes. There are actually four Dow Jones averages: the Industrial Average, which is made up of the 30 stocks listed in the previous question; the Transportation Average, which is made up of 20 transportation stocks; the Utility Average, which is made up of 15 utility stocks; and the Composite Average, which is made up of the other three together. However, the most widely quoted and the one that you probably should be watching is the Dow Jones Industrial Average.

What is the S&P 500?

Many people believe that the 50-plus-year-old Standard and Poor's 500 (S&P 500) index gives a far more accurate picture of the general performance of the market than the DJIA, since it measures not just 30 but approximately 500 stocks of the largest American companies. The S&P 500 selects and tracks stocks on the basis of their trustworthiness, liquidity, and sector representation. Almost as widely quoted as the DJIA, the S&P 500 differs not only in the number of representative stocks it tracks, but also in its calculations, which, unlike the Dow's, are "market-weighted." This means that each stock's influence in the index mirrors its market value (the price of the stock multiplied by the number of outstanding shares).

What is the Wilshire 5000 Total Market Index?

The Wilshire 5000 Total Market Index represents the broadest index for the U.S. equity market, measuring the performance of all U.S.-headquartered equity securities, with readily available price data. The index was named after the nearly 5,000 stocks it contained when it was originally created, but it has grown to include over 5,700 stocks.

What is the Wilshire 4500 Index?

Take the number of stocks on the Wilshire 5000 Total Market

Index, subtract most of the companies that appear on the S&P 500 Index, and you will have the Wilshire 4500 Index. Medium and small capitalization managers use the Wilshire 4500 as a performance benchmark.

What is the Russell 3000 Index?

The Russell Index, which, like the S&P 500, is market-weighted, tracks the performance of some 3,000 large-cap U.S. companies.

What is the Russell 2000 Index?

This index takes the 2,000 smallest stocks on the Russell 3000 and gives them an index of their own. (Remember, "smallest" here is a relative term, given the size and stability of the securities tracked by the bigger Russell 3000.)

What is the Schwab 1000 Index?

This market-weighted index comprises the 1,000 biggest publicly traded securities in America, including General Electric, Microsoft, Intel, Exxon, and Wal-Mart Stores.

What is the S&P MidCap 400 Index?

Like the S&P 500, the S&P MidCap 400 Index is market-weighted and made up of stable, liquid companies with strong industry representation. Unlike the S&P 500, this index comprises 400 mid-cap securities.

What is the S&P SmallCap 600 Index?

The market-weighted S&P SmallCap 600 Index is made up of 600 small-cap stocks, again selected for their stability, liquidity, and industry representation.

What is the Morgan Stanley Capital International Europe, Australia, Far East Index (MSCI EAFE)?

This index is made up of roughly 1,100 stocks traded on some 21 different exchanges from Europe to Asia-Pacific.

What is the NASDAQ index?

NASDAQ is not only an electronic stock market; it is also an index that tracks approximately 4,000 mostly technology-oriented stocks and that, like the S&P 500, is market-weighted, so that the largest stocks have more impact on the index level than smaller ones.

How do I know which of these various indexes is best for me?

To decide which index is the best benchmark for you to use (remember, it pays to measure your investments' performance against the value of an index), you must compare the stocks that make up various indexes to your holdings. Is your particular portfolio chock-a-block with large transportation securities, such as railroad and airplane stocks? Then it is worth your while to keep a close watch on the Dow Jones Transportation Average. If your portfolio is heavily weighted with utility securities, such as telephone, electricity, or natural gas stocks, then you should keep your eye on the Dow Jones Utility Average to get a good idea of how utility stocks are doing overall.

You can also use the indexes that match your holdings to find out how well, or how badly, your stocks performed during extreme economic times in our history, such as periods of inflation or recession, or even during the stock market crash of 1987.

What if the index that I'm following is doing well, but my stocks aren't keeping pace with it?

This is a sign that you need to do some serious investigation into why your stocks are underperforming. You might uncover some very valid reasons to consider selling some of your holdings and putting your money elsewhere.

Which index should I use to evaluate the overall health of the stock market?

I use all three of the biggies: the Dow Jones Industrial Average, the S&P 500, and the NASDAQ. And I use one that takes them all into consideration: the Wilshire 5000. If we are in a truly healthy market, then all will be doing well. But if one is doing well and the others are not, which is known as a divergence in the market, I take this as an early warning sign that the market might be weakening.

What if everything looks good for the stock I'm about to buy, but the overall market is doing very poorly? Would you advise me to buy that stock?

Another key indicator I consider before buying any stock is the overall direction of the market. If I feel that the market is about to turn bearish, I have to tell you, I would be reluctant to buy any stock, regardless of what an individual company is doing, unless I used a very handy investing technique called dollar cost averaging, which I'll say more about later.

What if the indexes show that the overall market is positive and I want to buy a stock, but the stock I'm interested in is hitting new highs? Does this mean I should not buy it?

No, but do your homework. Is everything else in line for the stock to go up further? Are the quarterly and annual earnings per share healthy and growing, is the volume strong, and is the company a market and an industry leader, with small institutional ownership? Is management good? Are the company's products diverse and new or updated? If so, then the stock's hitting a new high may be a positive sign.

INDUSTRY LEADERS

I always see in the paper that certain stocks are industry leaders. What does this mean?
An industry leader is typically a large-cap company that has a dominant position in its industry and creates a dominant product for that particular market. In other words, it leads all the companies in that industry.

How important is it that the stock I'm thinking about buying be a market and an industry leader?
In my opinion, very important. This is another of the key factors I look for before I buy a stock. I want my stocks to be market and industry leaders, and so should you.

MEASURING A STOCK'S VALUE

I want to know whether to buy a stock, and I know the financial pages of the newspaper can help me. But what do all those numbers mean?
The numbers won't seem so complicated if we go through them one by one. The first columns, headed "High" and "Low," list the highest and lowest prices paid for the stock in the past year. The "Stock" column shows the name of the stock in question, usually abbreviated. The figure under "Dividend" is typically an estimate of the dividend amount the

stock will pay based on recent past performance. "100s" tells you the number of shares sold for the day in question, or the trading volume, expressed in hundreds. (If 4,000,000 shares of a particular stock were traded that day, then under "100s" you would see "40,000.") Next you will see "High" and "Low" again. This time they refer to the highest and lowest prices paid for the stock during the business day in question. "Last" refers to the closing price, or the last trade of the stock that day, and "Change" reflects the difference between the closing price of the stock at the end of the session and the closing price the day before. You will also see the letters P/E. Those letters stand for the price/earnings ratio of the stock, which I'll explain later in this book.

What is one of the biggest pitfalls for people who buy stocks?

The biggest pitfall of all is that we tend not to watch the important predictors of a stock's performance *after* we have purchased it. We often thoroughly research a stock before we buy it, but then we slack off from performing ongoing research as we hold that stock. It is almost as if we want to believe blindly that the stock will be a success from the moment we buy it. But things change within a company, and a good investor has to monitor the changes as they happen.

What are some of the predictors that need to be monitored?

Here's a partial list: company revenues, earnings per share, price-earnings ratio, book value, daily trading volume, dividends, yield, debt, and volatility. Please note: While most people continue to watch a company's earnings per share to see how the company is performing relative to other, similar companies, that may not be the best available valuation method.

There are many subtle but achievable ways for a corporation to manipulate the information that makes up earnings. I would pay more attention to revenues.

REVENUES

What are revenues?

Revenues are simply the amount of money a corporation takes in from sales of its products and services from year to year. As you consider buying or holding a stock, keep an eye on whether the company's revenues are going up, remaining stable, or going down. That figure is very hard to manipulate.

P/E RATIO

What is a price/earnings ratio?

A price/earnings ratio (P/E ratio) is a basic and very useful measure of how well a corporation is performing. Here's an example of what it means: If the price of a stock is $40 a share and the company has earnings of $2 a share, the P/E ratio is 20 ($40 divided by $2, which equals 20).

The higher the P/E ratio, the riskier the stock is likely to be. The Internet stocks that everyone became familiar with in the 1990s had very high P/E ratios—or none at all, because most of these companies did not even have earnings to compute a P/E ratio with. A new breed of investors seemed not to be paying as much attention to P/E ratios as investors once did. Traditionally speaking, however, stocks with a low P/E ratio might be considered a good buy at their current market price. Why? Because if a stock currently has a low share price relative to its earnings and research shows that it is a good stock, then its price will probably eventually go up. (Remember the definition of a value stock?) Also, if a stock has a low P/E ratio and the market heads south, the price of that stock may not fall as much as the price of stocks with high P/E ratios.

I know the price of the stock I'm interested in. How can I find out the earnings per share to figure out what the P/E ratio is?

If all you want to know is the P/E ratio of a stock, check the newspaper. But it's a very good idea to know the earnings per share for other reasons—including that they measure profitability. To compute earnings per share, you take the net profits of the corporation after it has paid taxes and subtract any dividends due to preferred stockholders. (Remember, owners of preferred stock have a fixed dividend that must be paid before the owners of common stock receive any profits.) Divide that number by the number of outstanding shares of common stock, which you can find in the company's annual report, the company website, or a financial website.

Here's an example. Say that, after taxes, the Orman Corporation earned a net profit of $3,400,000 last year. It's time for the Orman Corporation to pay dividends to preferred stockholders, which come to $400,000. The Orman Corporation has 3,000,000 shares of common stock outstanding. After subtracting the preferred stock dividends from the net profit ($3,400,000 minus $400,000 equals $3,000,000), you divide the remaining number by the number of outstanding common shares ($3,000,000 divided by 3,000,000). The answer—$1.00 per share—represents the earnings per share. In other words, for every share of stock Orman Corporation has issued, it earned about $1.00 last year.

What does a company do with its earnings per share? Will I get them as a dividend, the way preferred shareholders do?

Possibly, but in most cases no. The company will keep those earnings to reinvest in its core businesses, or to acquire other companies that will help the company to grow.

Then why are earnings per share important?
Because if a company doesn't earn money, it can't grow (unless it borrows), people won't invest in it, and its stock price won't go up. If a company can't earn money for itself, chances are it won't earn money for you, either.

How often are the earnings of a corporation calculated?
Quarterly. This means a corporation makes the above calculations every three months to show if the company is meeting its projections for growth.

What kind of earnings per share should I be looking for in a company whose stock I want to buy?
That is a hard question to answer, because each stock is really in competition with itself. A corporation's goal is for its quarterly earnings to beat its earnings for the same quarter in the previous year and for its total annual earnings to beat the annual earnings of the year before. Remember, over the long term, earnings are what count to the market and to investors. Increases in earnings are a good sign.

How do I know if the stock I'm interested in has beat its earnings from last year?
The previous year's earnings (or earnings for the same quarter in the previous year) will be posted along with the current year's (or quarter's) earnings as soon as the current earnings are announced. If yours is a well-traded stock, these figures will appear in all major financial publications and financial websites.

When I see the earnings of a stock, how do I know if they are good or bad?

In my opinion, what you always want to see is that the stock's quarterly and annual earnings increased over the same quarter in the previous year.

When it comes to buying a stock, do only the current annual earnings per share matter?

Absolutely not! You also should be looking at past and future annual earnings and projections. For instance, with the Orman Corporation, you would want to see that the company has had good earnings growth over the past five years, and also that its earnings projections show a continued growth pattern. If earnings grow, so, probably, will the price of a company's stock.

If a stock that I have purchased continues to go up steadily, will the P/E ratio go higher as well?

Not necessarily. Remember, the P/E ratio is the current price of the stock divided by the current earnings of the company. If the company's earnings increase as rapidly, or more rapidly, than the price of the stock, then the P/E ratio could stay the same, or even decrease. But chances are, if the price of a stock goes up quickly, the P/E ratio will increase faster than the earnings of that company.

Should all price/earnings ratios for all categories of stocks be judged in the same way?

No. Each industry or economic sector has its own average P/E ratio. For instance, bank stocks sell at an average P/E ratio of 15 or 16, while energy stocks historically sell for an average P/E ratio of 25 or slightly higher. So which stock you own and which category it falls into will make a big difference in how you assess its particular P/E ratio. A P/E ratio that is average in one category could be high in another category.

How do I know what the average P/E ratio is for the kind of stock that I am interested in?

This information can be easily accessed over the Internet. For instance, Yahoo! Finance *(finance.yahoo.com)* will give you the average P/E ratios of all the different categories of stock.

Do stock markets themselves have average P/E ratios?

Yes. In April 2002, for example, the S&P 500 was selling at a P/E ratio of 45.61, the highest it has ever reached as of this writing. (This does not mean that it will not go higher.) The higher the P/E ratio of the market, the more speculative the market as a whole becomes.

PRICE/EARNINGS TO GROWTH

What is Price/Earnings to Growth?

Price/Earnings to Growth (PEG) is an indicator that compares the price/earnings ratio of a stock to the earnings growth of the company. What you want to see is a company whose earnings growth rate at least matches the P/E ratio of the stock. If the company's earnings are growing by 30 percent a year, for example, the stock's P/E ratio should be no more than 30. The PEG is, historically, a good indicator of value.

VOLUME

Why is it important to know how many shares of a stock have traded on a given day?

The trading volume of a stock on a given day tells you something about the current supply and demand of that stock.

Remember that if demand exceeds supply, this can push the price of the stock upward. If you happen to see a spike in volume, this could be an indicator that there is sudden interest in this stock—either to buy or to sell—from a large investor or from many, many smaller investors.

Are supply and demand key factors in buying a stock?

Yes. Besides the quarterly and annual earnings per share, I always look at the supply and demand of a stock before making a purchase. When there is great demand for a stock and very little of it available for sale, then its price will be pushed up faster than that of a stock that has lots of supply and very little demand.

What are you looking for when you look at the volume?

One of the things I like to see is an increase in volume as a stock starts to move upward in price. If a stock's price goes up on very little volume, one possible interpretation is that the move is not a solid one. But if the stock's price rises on strong volume, I would tend to take it as a sign that the move is a more solid one. An increase in volume on a rise in price says two things to me: Many people are interested in the stock (which is good) and/or institutions are starting to buy the stock in large blocks. A big movement on little volume suggests that a few people who think the stock is going to move were suckered into paying more for the stock than they probably had to.

What if the stock I'm interested in has very small volume—or on some days it does not trade at all?

This stock is what is known as an illiquid stock. It is most likely very speculative, and one that I would be very careful about buying. Illiquid stocks can be difficult to sell without taking a loss.

Book Value

Why do I need to know the book value of a stock?

The book value of a stock is a measure of the worth of the company's assets, including real estate, equipment, inventories, cash, etc., less the company's liabilities. It is also called equity or shareholders' equity. It is the supposed "true value" of that corporation on the books, based on the historical value of the company's assets and liabilities. It is also a rough approximation of the liquidation value of a corporation. The book value does not necessarily bear any relation to the stock price and, in most cases today, is not anywhere close to that number.

How do I find the book value of a stock?

Like the P/E ratio and all the other terms we're defining, book value is listed in newspapers and updated on every quoting service that you will find on the Web. Book value per share is calculated by dividing the total book value by the number of shares outstanding.

Is there a way of using book value in evaluating a stock?

Yes, there is—the price-to-book ratio. The price-to-book ratio is used to compare the price of one stock to that of another stock, or to the market as a whole, in terms of a company's underlying value. There are problems with this as a method of evaluation, which I'll get to in a moment, but you can calculate the price-to-book ratio by dividing the current per-share stock price by the book value per share. Investors searching for bargains try to buy stocks near, or below, their book value. Another technique is to search for stocks selling below the marketwide average book value.

Historically, price-to-book has been a key ratio for determining the value of a stock, and was often used in the stock selection process. It is still important when evaluating financial companies such as banks, brokerages, and credit card companies. In these industries, takeovers are priced based on a multiple of book value (usually between 1.75 and 2.0 times book value). It is also valuable for industrial companies that have significant capital assets. The value of these assets often places a floor under the stock price. You should know, however, that price-to-book may be less useful when valuing today's service and technology stocks. A software giant like Microsoft produces high-margin products without a significant investment in either real estate or capital equipment. As a result, Microsoft's book value is relatively low. Another problem with the price-to-book ratio concept is that one of the terms—book value—is so easily manipulated. Valuation of inventory and real estate are easily adjusted on the books. Stock buybacks and write-offs of exceptional items also deflate book value, making high-priced stocks seem overvalued.

DIVIDENDS

I know that dividends are distributions of a company's earnings to shareholders, but when are they paid out?
Every three months companies report their earnings, but only some of them send out dividends, or quarterly cash payments, to their shareholders. Companies are not obligated to do this. If a company is experiencing a hard time, dividends are usually the first thing to go.

How are dividends taxed?
Dividends are now taxed at the same rate as capital gains: 15 percent for most taxpayers, only 5 percent for those in the two lowest income tax brackets, at least until 2010, when the rate

on dividends is due to revert to ordinary income tax rates. Since dividends used to be taxed as ordinary income, with a top rate of over 35 percent, they are more attractive to investors than they were just a few years ago. But remember the tax rate is due to revert in 2010.

I'm thinking about taking money out of my CDs and investing in dividend-paying stock so I can get a higher yield and pay less taxes. Do you think this is a good idea?

Well, you are doing exactly what the government would like you to do. When interest rates are fairly low, as they were in the year 2006, we are all being forced out of our safe hiding places, like CDs, into dividend-paying stocks that will give us more bang for the buck. I think dividend-paying stocks are a smart way to get more income, but you need to be careful. Unlike your bank CD or money-market fund, stock values can go down. So if you use dividend-paying stocks to get a better income payment, promise me that you will watch your investment carefully to make sure the stock does not tank.

Is a dividend the only thing to which I may be legally entitled as a shareholder?

No. As an owner of common stock, you are entitled to vote on matters of corporate policy. Granted, small investors have practically no influence on who the next CEO of the company is going to be, but by law companies have to involve you in the decision-making process, usually by allowing you to vote for members of their board of directors and on proposals that are before the board of directors (and shareholders can make proposals, too). Also, in the event that the company files for bankruptcy and must liquidate its assets, you as a shareholder have the right to share in the company's assets after its debts have been discharged.

YIELD

What is my yield on a stock?
Yield is your return, in the form of dividends, on the shares of stock that you own. It is expressed as a percentage. Your yield percentage is based on what you paid for the stock when you bought it—not, please note, on its current trading price.

Where can I find the current yield of a stock?
In the newspaper or on the Web. You also can compute the current yield of a stock yourself by taking the current market price of a share—say, $25—and dividing it by the current annual dividend per share, say, $1.50. This stock would yield you around 6 percent a year.

When I look in the papers, it seems as if the yield of a stock changes every day. Why?
The yield is determined by the current market price of the stock and the annual dividend that particular stock pays. So even though the annual dividend, when there is one, tends to stay the same, the price of the stock changes on a daily basis, which causes the listed yield to change.

Does that mean that even after I buy a stock, my yield can change?
Yes, if the annual dividend changes. Once you have purchased a stock, you are locked in at your purchase price. No matter what the market price of the stock may be, your yield will be based on what you paid for the stock, so the only way your yield can change is if the dividend changes.

Why is it important to know what the yield is?

People who buy stocks for income rather than growth need to know what the return, or yield, on those stocks is or is going to be. For example, you may find two stocks you like, but one has a yield of 6.5 percent and the other has a yield of 2 percent. This difference is significant if you need the money to live on. Yield also may tell you if it's wise to keep your money in a particular stock or not.

Let's say that in your Roth IRA you hold 500 shares of a stock that you bought when the share price was $10. You made an investment of $5,000. At the time you invested, the current yield on this stock was 6 percent, or $0.60 a share. This means your yearly dividends would amount to $0.60 a share times 500 shares, or $300 a year; your dividend divided by your initial investment ($300 divided by $5,000) gives you your yield: 6 percent. Three years later, the stock has gone up to $50 a share. Your $5,000 investment is now worth $25,000. But your annual dividend (and, of course, your original purchase price and number of shares) has stayed the same, so you are still getting just $0.60 a share, or $300 a year. (Meanwhile, new investors would only be getting about a 1.2 percent yield on their money—an annual dividend of $0.60 divided by the share price of $50.) Given that your money has grown considerably and since income is your objective, you might decide to sell the stock, cash in on the profits, and reinvest this money in a higher-yielding investment. So you sell the stock for $25,000. (Because it was in your Roth IRA, you do not have to pay capital-gains taxes on this money.) You invest all $25,000 in a stock that is yielding you 6 percent. Because your capital investment is five times your original investment, your current income also increases by a factor of five: from $300 a year to $1,500. Big difference for you—more than $100 a month.

Please note: Even if you owned this stock outside of a

retirement account and you had to pay capital-gains tax on the gain, it still might be worth it. For instance, in the scenario above, you would owe taxes on the $20,000 profit you made ($25,000 minus $5,000 equals $20,000) at the capital-gains rate of 15 percent. This means you would owe $3,000 in taxes. This would leave you with $22,000 to invest after taxes. If you invested this $22,000 in a new stock or bond that was yielding you 6 percent, this would still give you $1,320 a year of income. If current income is your goal, this is still much better than the $300 you were getting, in spite of the capital-gains tax you had to pay.

If I'm not that interested in getting current income, is there any other reason I would buy stocks that pay dividends?

It depends on what the markets are doing and how you feel about your money possibly just sitting there, doing nothing. Many people who do not need current income like having a stock that pays them a dividend for two reasons. One is that they like to reinvest that dividend in more shares of the same stock as a way of accumulating shares. Second, when a market is going down and you see your stock shrinking in value, sometimes it is not so painful when you know that at least you are getting a good yield on your money.

I have been told that there is an investment strategy that has to do with buying stocks based on yield that will give me good growth on my money. Can you tell me what that is?

This is a popular investment strategy named Dogs of the Dow—in other words, buying the stocks that are currently considered the dogs (the ones not performing) of the Dow Jones Industrial Average. "Dog" status is determined by a stock's yield. If you were to use this strategy, you would start by finding out which 10 stocks of the Dow were currently offering the highest yield, and you would buy them in equal amounts. One year later, you would look at all 30 stocks of the Dow again, and again you would see which 10 stocks were currently offering the highest yield. You would then adjust your portfolio accordingly. You do this every year, and in theory, over time these Dogs of the Dow will rise in price and outperform the market.

Do the Dogs of the Dow always outperform the market?
In recent years the dogs have actually underperformed the market, so many people are trying to tweak the strategy and make it work again. Some people are buying 5 stocks rather than 10.

VOLATILITY

The volatility of a stock—how rapidly and dramatically its price rises and falls relative to the overall stock market—is tracked with a measurement known as beta. A stock with a beta of 1 is projected to move in direct correlation to the overall stock market. So if the market goes up or down 10 percent, this stock should also move up or down 10 percent. Anything greater than 1 and you are looking at a stock that will experience more dramatic moves than the overall market. If a stock has a beta of 1.5, it should move up or down about 50 percent more than the overall market. So if the market is up 10 percent, this stock should be up 15 percent, and if the market is down 10 percent, this stock will be down 15 percent.

What if my stock has a beta less than 1?
If you have a beta of 0.5, then your stock has been 50 percent less volatile than the market. A negative beta (say, -1) means

that a stock moves inversely to the overall market, so when the market rises, the stock goes down, and vice versa.

Why is it important to know the beta of a stock?

When you know the beta of a stock (along with other information you have gathered) you can determine if that particular stock is one that you will feel comfortable owning, given your risk tolerance. Let's say you think the market is going to go way up and you want to take full advantage of that movement, so you have decided to invest in aggressive growth stocks. With this in mind, you might feel comfortable owning stocks whose betas are greater than 1. Theoretically, if the market goes on a major upward tear, your stock will outperform the market. But please remember that the higher the beta, the more money the stock can potentially lose. The lower the beta, the less you will participate in an upward market, but the less risk you'll have if the market heads south.

DEBT-TO-EQUITY RATIO

It's important to check out how much debt a company carries, traditionally measured by the debt-to-equity ratio. Here, you are looking for a low figure, less than 1. If the ratio is greater than 2, this means the company has a lot of outstanding debt for its size and therefore a lot of interest to pay on its debt. If the company ever needs money, the interest will come out of the stockholders' equity. You don't want this to happen.

What should I know about the debt that a company carries?

You should be concerned about the kind as well as the amount of debt a company carries. Like people, corporations can carry both good and bad debt. Good debt is the kind you carry as an investment in the years to come. Bad debt is the kind that drags you down and keeps you from investing wholeheartedly in the future.

Has a company incurred debt in order to finance its growth? Or is it in so much debt that it cannot possibly sustain future growth? Debt is something to keep a watchful eye on when you buy or own shares in a company.

I bought a stock that was an industry leader, had great revenues, rising profits and sales, and a very low P/E ratio in comparison to the S&P index, which is the main reason I bought it. It was off 25 percent from its high for the year. Now it's falling. What did I miss?

This is known as the value trap. You think that something is well priced, but as the price continues to fall, you suspect that this was no bargain after all. Usually, what has happened is that the main indicator you are watching is the stock price. But you should never buy a stock based on price, or even on P/E, alone. You should always purchase a stock based on its revenues, earnings, projected future earnings, whether it's an industry and market leader, and where the economy is, among other things. And when considering the P/E ratio, remember: The key factor that is *not* measured in a P/E ratio is debt. And as you know, debt is a very important part of the equation. You always want to look at the debt of a company as well as the P/E ratio before buying.

How do I use enterprise value?

This indicator is best used when comparing stocks within the same industry, to see if the stocks are fairly valued.

INSTITUTIONAL INVESTORS

An institutional investor is a major player—for example, a mutual fund company, an insurance company, or a government pension plan—with the resources to invest huge sums of money in the stock market as a whole or in any one particular stock at a given time. Institutional investors account for the majority of overall trading volume on most exchanges.

Why is it important for me to know what institutional investors are saying and doing about my stock?

Because what they say and do can have a major impact on the price of your stock and on the direction of the markets. In fact, when I'm interested in a stock, the number of institutional investors who own that stock is one of the key indicators I look for. But I don't always follow their lead. Sometimes I'm attracted by a stock that is not yet owned by many institutional investors, because if and when they discover the stock, their money can move its price upward significantly. The converse is also true: If there are a lot of institutional investors in a stock, and if they turn sour on it and get out, that could leave you with a big loss.

Where do I find out if my stock is currently being bought or sold by institutional investors?

An easy way to find this information is to look at the accumulation/distribution rating of your stock in a newspaper called the *Investor's Business Daily,* or to check the institutional investors section under your stock on one of the larger financial websites.

What does accumulation/distribution rating mean?

This rating tells you if your stock is under selling pressure or if it is the new sweetheart on the street when it comes to institutional investors. Remember, the more investors who buy, or who want to buy, your stock, the more its price will tend to go up; the more people who sell, or who want to sell, your stock, the more its price will tend to go down. The accumulation/distribution rating is usually based on an evaluation of the stock's daily price and volume action over the past 13 weeks of trading.

The scale consists of letters A through E-minus. A means that institutions are buying or accumulating a particular stock very heavily, but not selling it. As the letters move toward E-minus, the proportion of buying to selling decreases. C is what I call the midpoint, for it represents an equal amount of buying and selling. When you reach E-minus, this means very heavy selling, or distribution, and very light buying.

ANNUAL REPORTS

I recently sent away for the annual report of a company I'm interested in investing in. What should I look for as I read?
Among the things I would want to know are: How old is the company? If it's a new, untested company, I would be extremely wary. I'd also want to know who's in charge of the company. Who is the chief executive officer (CEO), and has he or she been on the job for a while or is he or she newly appointed? Is poor leadership reflected in the company's past performance? Is the company profitable, and if so, how quickly are its profits growing year to year? Is it expanding its customer base, or is that base shrinking? What new products or services does the company have in its pipeline? Are there special challenges or opportunities that lie ahead for the year to come?

How can I find out if a company is profitable or not?
Profits for the past year will be itemized in the corporate annual report. You can also request this information by calling or writing the company directly, or find the statistics you seek—including revenues, expenses, profits, and debts—on

the company's website. When looking at profitability, try to go back at least five years, ten if you can. You want to make sure that the company has shown a consistent level—or, better yet, growth—of profits over the years.

ANALYSIS

Many indicators and signals can be used to analyze a stock. The two most widely talked about forms of analysis are fundamental analysis and technical analysis.

What is fundamental analysis?

Fundamental analysis is simply a way of evaluating whether a company's stock is financially sound based on the following information: how long the company's management has been in place and its record, the company's chief competitors and the competitive environment, the chances of its scoring big with a new product, and whether it will have good earnings. Simply put, no matter how the stock of a company is trading, analysts are looking to see if the company is fundamentally sound—not only today but also for the future. The downside of this type of analysis? A lot of people believe it is based on information that most investors can get hold of, and so it is nothing special. Also, many financial experts believe that the kind of conclusions you can draw from this kind of analysis are soft—that is, not particularly objective, or provable.

What is technical analysis?

Technical analysis is more concerned with market patterns and trends than with the dollars-and-cents fundamentals of a company. For example, it uses historical stock-price charts to see how high a stock's price can rise, or how far it can fall, before the stock's movement meets what's called resistance—the point at which the stock price is likely to switch direction and start heading down, or up, again.

I have been monitoring a stock that the technical analysts on TV said was a good buy at 50. It went down to 25, and I thought that made it a great buy. I bought it, and it's now sitting in my portfolio at 10. What happened?

I'm sorry to say that many individual investors think just as you do. If a stock is a good investment at X, it must be twice as good when the price is ½X. Wrong, wrong, wrong.

We saw this phenomenon in spades during the dot-com gold rush of the '90s, and stock analysts are very much to blame, if you ask me. How many analysts changed the opinions they were offering on some of those stocks whose prices plummeted by 50 percent, 60 percent, 70 percent, and more? Not many. The lesson: You have to know when to buy or sell based on your own analysis and not rely on a group of people who far too often react to news long after it is too late. That said, keep your eyes on the fundamental and technical warning signs.

INVESTING TECHNIQUES FOR EVERYONE

THE BENEFITS OF DOLLAR COST AVERAGING

I am afraid that the market may go down after I start investing. Needless to say, I do not want to lose money. What can I do to limit my exposure?

Assuming that the investments in your account are good, sound, and just going up and down due to the volatility of the market, you can use a technique I love, called dollar cost averaging. Dollar cost averaging is an excellent way to guard against paying too much for stocks in a volatile market. Here's how it works. You invest exactly the same dollar amount at regular intervals (preferably every month) into a specific investment vehicle or vehicles. This method actually *averages out* the price you pay for your shares, and puts time, your money, and the market all on your side, regardless of what your stock or the market does over the short term.

Why should I spread my investment over time? Why don't I just wait until the market is at the bottom and put all my money in then?

What you are suggesting is called timing the market: buying low and selling high. It's a wonderful trick if you can pull it off. But most people can't. A lot of people have lost a lot of money trying to outfox the market.

Can you show me the dollars-and-cents advantages of dollar cost averaging?

Yes. Consider this comparison of buying stock all at once, with a lump sum of money, and buying the same stock gradually, over time:

Outright Purchase

Let's say you have $12,000 you want to invest, and you know which stock you want to buy. You have been watching your stock for some time, and you have seen it go as high as $15 a share. Recently, it has taken a tumble to $10. You think to yourself, now is the time to buy. You invest all $12,000 at once by making an outright purchase of 1,200 shares at $10 a share. For the first three weeks you are happy, since the share price is staying at about $10, but all of a sudden the market as a whole turns down, and you watch the price of your shares start to decline. You still think this stock is a great investment and don't want to sell, because when the market turns around your stock will come back, too. One year later, your stock is selling at $5 a share. You are down $5 a share, and you now have a paper loss of $6,000 on your 1,200 shares.

Dollar Cost Averaging

If you had taken that same $12,000 and invested it using dollar cost averaging, you would have divided up your lump sum and invested the same percentage of it, or the same sum of money, month in, month out, regardless of what the market was doing—in this example, $1,000 per month. And here is how you would have come out in the same scenario. (See the chart on page 59.)

As you can see, by using dollar cost averaging, you are able to buy *more shares* of stock when the price is low, and therefore more shares overall. After one year, instead of having 1,200 shares you have 1,717 shares, and even though the price per share is still down, at $5 per share your holdings are worth $8,585 instead of $6,000 and your loss on paper is only $3,415, or about $2,585 less than if you had purchased the stock outright.

Comparison:
$3,415 loss with dollar cost averaging
$6,000 loss with outright purchase

But there is continuing good news when you use dollar cost averaging instead of making an outright purchase.

Let's say that after a year, you decide you don't want to invest any more money in your stock but just want to wait and see what happens to it. So you leave your $12,000 invested and become an observer.

Dollar Cost Averaging: An Example

MONTH	PRICE	SHARES BOUGHT
1	$10	100
2	$9	111
3	$8	125
4	$7	143
5	$8	125
6	$9	111
7	$6	167
8	$8	125
9	$7	143
10	$6	167
11	$5	200
12	$5	200

TOTAL: $12,000 invested; 1,717 shares bought

Eighteen months later, the market starts to go back up, and slowly but surely the price of the stock you purchased inches back up to $10 a share. With an outright purchase, you bought 1,200 shares, so when the price returns to $10 you've broken even—your investment is now worth what you originally paid for it, $12,000. But using dollar cost averaging, you would have accumulated 1,717 shares, or 517 more than with an outright purchase. In this scenario, when your per-share price goes back up to $10, your 1,717 shares will be worth $17,170. This is $5,170 more than your original $12,000 investment, or about a 43 percent return on your money. With dollar cost averaging, you limit your loss in a down market, and when the price per share rises again, you also make more. Again, the key to this technique is that you are always buying additional shares of your investment at a lower price, as the chart shows.

I can see now that in a down market I can limit my losses with dollar cost averaging. But what if we are just coming out of a bear market and the bull is starting to make its run? Wouldn't I be better off investing everything I have at once?

If you are sure that this is the investment scenario, then of course you would be better off investing everything at once. The problem for most of us is that we do not know whether the bull is about to gallop, or merely take a few steps and graze or backtrack. If you feel you can judge this, then go for it. Otherwise, over the long run you will be better off using dollar cost averaging.

DRIPs

I hear people talking about DRIPs. What are they?

DRIP stands for dividend reinvestment program. The DRIP program started in the 1950s as a way for employees of corporations to accumulate stock in the companies they were working for. If the employee chose, every time the company paid a dividend, that dividend could be reinvested back into the employee's account to buy more shares of stock. This was usually done with very low—or no—commissions or fees, which made these programs quite cost-efficient. As time went on, many corporations decided to open up their DRIP programs to all their investors. Today, DRIP programs are offered by about 1,300 U.S. and foreign companies, and are open to almost anyone (employees or otherwise) who wants to buy the stock.

How do DRIPs work?

After you have purchased at least one share of stock of a company that offers a DRIP program, you can continue to buy shares or partial shares of stock in that company by instructing the company to reinvest your dividends and/or by sending the company money, in some cases in amounts as small as $10, $20, or $25. Money that you send in is known as an optional cash payment, or an OCP. Currently, about 100 DRIP companies will also offer you a discount on their stock, anywhere from 3 percent to 5 percent off the stock's current market price.

If I can find a stock in the DRIP program that gives me a 3 to 5 percent discount on my purchase, isn't this a good way to go?
Yes, if you like the stock. But please note that not many plans offer this discount. If you find one that does, please ask whether the plan offers that discount on any optional cash payments you may make. Many companies give you a discount only on shares purchased with reinvested dividends.

I've heard that in order to send in optional cash payments, I have to reinvest my dividends in the DRIP program. Is this true?
Many companies permit optional cash payments only if the shareholder participates in the DRIP (reinvests), but some companies do allow shareholders to receive all dividend payments and still participate in the optional payment feature of the plan.

Does it matter when I send in my OCPs?
It could. You should make it a point to find out when the corporation actually invests the money you send. For example, some DRIPs invest your money only every three months, or quarterly, but most DRIPs specify a monthly date when they make investments using your money. If that date is the 20th of every month, and you send in an OCP on the 2nd of every

month, your money will just be sitting there for 18 days, doing no work and earning no interest for you.

Do all DRIP programs allow me to send in any amount of money I want whenever I want?

No. Each DRIP program has its own set of rules. Many DRIPs require an initial minimum investment from $250 to $1,000 or require you to buy a minimum number of shares. Be aware, too, that the program may charge fees to maintain the account.

Are the fees and expenses the same among all DRIP programs?

No. Fees, especially fees associated with selling the stock you have purchased, differ. DRIPs are becoming so popular that many companies are charging new and higher fees to maintain these programs. You can be charged an enrollment fee and a transaction fee, plus a fee every time you buy shares. On the other hand, there are still a number of companies that charge minimal or no fees.

Can you name a few of the companies that do not charge fees or require high minimum investments?

As of the writing of this book, the following companies charge no fees and only require a purchase of one share to get started:

Coca-Cola
Hasbro
Harley-Davidson
Intel
Johnson & Johnson
Kellogg's
Wendy's

Are there other good companies in addition to the ones listed on the previous page that offer DRIPs?

Yes. The program is offered by many of the best companies in the world. In fact, almost all of the Dow Jones Industrial Average stocks offer dividend reinvestment programs. There is no shortage of quality stocks for DRIP investors. A fairly comprehensive list of DRIPs can be found at *www.dripadvisor.com.*

What companies have steep entrance fees that I need to watch out for?

Two of the most popular DRIPs with steep fees are Disney and McDonald's. Each has a minimum purchase to start: You must initially buy at least ten shares, or invest at least $1,000 for Disney or $500 for McDonalds. They also charge you a setup fee that can be $5 to $15. Disney charges you a $5 transaction fee and requires each purchase, or OCP, to be at least $100. So, as you can see, knowing what the company is charging can tell you if it is worthwhile to buy directly—which in the case of Disney it is not—or instead to buy through a discount brokerage firm.

Are DRIPs a good way to dollar cost average?

Yes. Whether you invest with OCPs or through dividend reinvestment, or both, you are making good use of the dollar cost averaging technique.

How do I get started with a DRIP?

In most cases, to get started with a DRIP you must own at least one share of stock. (There are independent companies through which you can buy a single share of stock in any company to begin DRIP investing.) From that point on, you can send money to make additional purchases. Contact the DRIP plan administrator or the investor relations department in the company you are interested in. He or she will send you an application, which you will fill out and send back. Later, if you want to sell your shares, contact the same plan administrator, who will send you additional forms on which you will note the number of shares you wish to sell and the exact day on which you wish the sale to take place.

Can you name some of the independent companies or organizations that will let me buy one share of stock to begin DRIP investing?

The National Association of Investors Corporation is one such organization, reachable toll-free at (877) 275-6242 or online at *www.betterinvesting.org.* Another company is Temper Enrollment Service, at (800) 388-9993 or *www.directinvesting. com.* There's also First Share, at (800) 683-0743 or *www .firstshare.com*, and One Share, at (888) 777-6919 or *www .oneshare.com.* You can also buy a share of stock through an online brokerage firm.

If I decide to buy one share of stock through an online brokerage firm, how much should that cost?

Many online brokers today are willing to execute a trade for any amount of stock (that means one share—or more, if you want more) for about $5 to $15 per trade. At that cost it pays to go straight through an online company to buy or sell your stock.

Two of the best, as of the writing of this book, are Muriel Siebert, reachable at (800) 872-0444 or online at *www .m.siebernet.com,* and TD Ameritrade, at (800) 934-4448 or *www.tdameritrade.com.* You do not need a minimum investment to open an account, which is important if all you are doing is buying a share or two of stock. The price to make an online trade here will be about $10 to $15.

Are there any books that can help me to learn more about DRIPs?

Yes. In my opinion, two of the best are *Buying Stocks Without a Broker* and *No-Load Stocks* by Charles Carlson.

Can I invest in or find out more about DRIPs online?

Yes. You can do so through a few sites. One that I like is *www.netstockdirect.com.*

Do DRIPs have a downside?

Overall, DRIPs are a great way for the small investor to get started. Not all companies offer DRIPs, which can limit the stocks you invest in, but you do have a choice of most of the blue-chip stocks. The main drawback of investing in DRIPs not purchased directly with a brokerage firm is that you may have to sell your stock through the mail, and this can take some time. When you own a stock in a brokerage firm account, you can sell it in seconds if you need to. Not only will you get your money faster, you can also time the market better.

ASSET ALLOCATION

What is asset allocation?

Asset allocation is a fancy way of saying diversification, and it's one of the very first things you should think about when you begin to invest your money. Asset allocation is expressed in percentages: What percentage of my assets do I want to put in growth stocks, what percentage do I want to put in value stocks, what percentage do I want to put in bonds and cash equivalents, real estate, gold, and so on. Many people simply divvy up their money between stocks and bonds, but you can get as specific as you want to—for example, in stocks alone you can invest in aggressive stocks, large-cap stocks, small-cap stocks, international stocks, emerging market stocks, and global stocks.

The types of investments you choose to diversify into are important, and so is the amount of money you put into each investment category. After you have figured out your investment objectives and the kind of instruments you want to place your money in, then you have to decide how much money you should put into each kind of investment. This is asset allocation. Not only is asset allocation a time-honored technique for spreading investment risk over many competing classes of investment, it is also an important method of safeguarding your assets as you get older and your investment objectives change.

How do I determine the appropriate allocation of my assets?

At this point, we return to a very basic question: How much risk are you willing to take? What happens if your portfolio takes a dive? Will you be able to resist the impulse to bail out? The amount of risk you are comfortable with is a fundamental factor in your decisions about how to allocate your money.

Another basic element in decision making is your age. One rule of thumb is that you subtract your age from 110 and the difference is the percentage of your assets that you should invest for growth. For instance, if you are 40 years old, subtract 40 from 110, which gives you 70; by this reasoning you should be putting 70 percent of your investment assets into growth-oriented investments while keeping 30 percent safe and sound (e.g., in bonds). Your age is important because it determines your investment horizon. But many other factors also come into play: your comfort with risk, your employment outlook, your family situation, and your current goals—e.g., whether you want to buy a home and will need money for a down payment.

I'm 25 years old and I'm saving to buy a home in the next two years. All of my money is in a money-market fund to be used for a down payment. I was recently told that I am too young to keep that money where it is and that I need to allocate better. Do you agree?

No. The amount of time you have before you need your investment money is crucial. Is it five years? Ten years? If so, you can invest in the market. But if you will need your money in one, two, or three years, then a money-market fund is the right place to have it. This is why asset-allocation models based on age do not always work. You know the specifics of your situation, so do what is best for you.

NOT FOR EVERYONE: SELLING SHORT

I've been hearing about "selling short" all my life. What does it mean?

Selling short is a stock market technique that is applied by the most sophisticated investors. It is used when an investor thinks a certain stock is about to go down and wants to profit from the downward movement of that stock. Now, when people want to profit from a market they think is going up, they try to buy shares of a stock low and sell high. But when people want to profit from a market going down, they do the reverse. They sell high first, and then hope to buy back lower. In other words, they are selling something before they have bought it, so they are said to be shorting the stock. It is one of the riskiest ways to make money in the stock market, and unless you're a very savvy investor, I would stay away from it.

WHEN TO SELL A STOCK

What are some indicators that tell me when it is time to sell?

The first thing that I always look at is the overall market. If the stock market is not on your side, that's one indicator that you might consider selling out of your stock position—after taking into consideration any tax ramifications. It's worth noting again, however, that if you're in the market for the long term and own a great stock but are not sure what to do, it's probably best to wait out a downturn.

How can I tell if the market downturn will be short- or long-term?

There are four major factors that direct the movement of the stock market: inflation, interest rates, the stability and profitability of key companies, and political affairs. The short answer is that there is no sure way to predict the market.

If the market is strong but my stock is going down, when should I call it quits and sell?

My own rule is that if a stock I own goes down 7 to 10 percent or more from the price I paid for it while the overall market is going up and other, similar stocks are either staying stable or going up, I am out of that stock.

What if I sell when the stock is down 8 percent, and then it turns around and goes back up?

Stick to your rules. If you don't, there will come a time, as we all saw in 2001 and 2002, when the stock goes from $200 to

50 cents. Contemplate the following fact, and remember it: When a stock goes down 50 percent, it has to go back up 100 percent for you to break even.

What do you mean, if a stock goes down 50 percent it has to go up 100 percent for me to break even?
This is what I mean. If you buy a stock for $20 a share and it goes down to $10 a share, that is a 50 percent decline. For that stock to go from $10 back to $20 is a 100 percent increase. It is harder for a stock to go up than to go down.

What are some other signs that I should take into consideration when thinking about selling my stock?
There are many, but here are three easy ones for you to watch for:

1. Volume. Watch the daily volume of shares that trade in your stock. When you see the volume increasing dramatically at the same time that the price of the stock is falling, take that as a danger sign.
2. Future earnings. If the projected quarterly earnings/revenues are threatening a slowdown, this is a bad sign.
3. Splits. When a company distributes more stock to holders of existing stock, that is called a stock split. For example, a 2-for-1 stock split means that for every share you held before the split, you now hold two, and each share will be worth half of its pre-split value. I feel wary when a stock splits too many times too quickly. If a stock splits two or three times in less than a year, I take this as a warning sign.

Is there a technical indicator that I can use to help me make an emotional decision on when to sell a stock or not buy it at all?

Yes. One of my favorite indicators is the 200-day moving average. This is simply an average of the closing price of a particular stock each day, recorded over a period of 200 days. If you chart those closing prices, you will get a line that, in my opinion, can serve as a key indicator of when to sell a stock. If a stock you own breaks below its own 200-day moving average, this can be a key signal to sell the stock. Many major financial websites let you view the 200-day moving averages for the stocks you own or in which you are interested.

Why is it that I always sell too soon?

Probably because of your fear that you will lose the profits that you see on paper. And we never like to lose.

But why do many of us feel we have to sell all or none of our shares of a stock? If you have made a tidy profit and you believe your stock may continue to rise, sell 25 percent of what you own. Or take out the dollar equivalent of your original investment plus maybe 10 percent of your profit, and then let your additional profits ride and see what happens. The same is true on the downside. If a stock starts to go down beyond your comfort level but you still have faith in the company and the stock, sell some of it. If it keeps going down, sell some more. Don't let your fear of loss keep you from a gain.

If I sell my stock because it has gone down 8 percent, do I go back in the market or do I stay out?

It depends on the overall direction of the market. If we are in a down market, it makes absolutely no sense to buy a stock, watch it go down 8 percent, sell it, and then buy another stock and watch it slide 8 percent. For when the direction of the market is down, it usually takes everything with it. So if you have an 8 percent loss and the overall market is going down, I would sell and stay on the sidelines with your cash. But if you've got an 8 percent loss on your stock and the overall market trend is up, then take your proceeds and reinvest the money in the rising market.

Why do you say I should sell a stock at an 8 percent loss? I have heard that a great way to invest is dollar cost averaging. I'm confused.

Dollar cost averaging is a fabulous technique when you have additional sums of money to invest month in and month out for a long period of time. Sometimes, however, you may have a lump sum of money, let's say $25,000, and you decide to invest it all at once in one stock. In that instance I think it makes sense to sell if the investment falls 8 percent.

So are you saying that if I am investing every month in my 401(k) plan and I still have at least 20 or 30 years until I need this money, that I should continue to invest as the market goes down?

That's exactly what I'm saying. As long as time is on your side, and you are in good quality investments such as diversified mutual funds within your 401(k) plan, you should just keep dollar cost averaging. Remember, the more the market goes down, the more the shares of your mutual funds decline in price and the more shares your contributions will buy. The more shares you own, the more money you make when it goes back up.

I understand how dollar cost averaging works when a market is going down, but is there a different technique if the market is going up?

Yes, it's a technique known as pyramiding. It is the strategy of adding to your initial stock purchase in smaller quantities, up to 5 percent, as the price of your stock increases. This is how it works: Once you determine the amount of money you can invest in a stock—let's use $10,000 as an example—use half ($5,000) to purchase one stock as your initial buy. If the stock goes down in price, don't buy any more. If the stock goes down 8 percent from the initial buy price, cut your losses and sell all of the stock as soon as possible.

If the stock increases 2 percent or 3 percent in price from your initial buy, and if you like how the stock is performing, consider buying $3,250 more. You would then have $8,250 of the $10,000 you are interested in investing in the one stock. If the stock increases 2 percent or 3 percent more, you can invest the remaining $1,750.

Now stop buying that stock and give the stock some time to grow. My recommendation is to buy and monitor: Monitor every stock or fund you own, and keep it only if it is still a good investment. Stocks and funds are just like relationships. You get into them because they are good, and when they are no longer good, you leave. You don't stay in a relationship because it *was* good, you stay in it because it *is* good. So constantly ask yourself if this is a stock or fund that you want to stay in a committed relationship with. A simple test is to ask yourself if you would buy it today. Never add money unless your prior buys seem to be working.

I'm holding stocks and mutual funds that have gone down 50 percent in value, and I don't have a clue if I should sell them or keep them. Can you help me? I don't want to sell them, because I don't want to take the loss. What is your opinion: Should I sell or hold on to them? If I were you, I would make a list of every investment that I currently own and write down the value that investment is worth today. I would then ask myself the question: If I did not currently own that investment but I had that money in cash, would I take that exact same amount of money and buy the investment that I am currently holding? If the answer to that question is no, sell that investment. If the answer is yes, then hold it. And if the answer is I don't know, sell half. It is really that simple.

GAINS

What do investors mean when they talk about realized gains and unrealized gains?

A realized gain is your profit on the capital you've invested, which you take by selling a security that has gone up in value since you purchased it. It is taxable. An unrealized gain means that your stock has gone up in value but you have not sold it. Therefore, you have not actually cashed in on, or realized, the gain. Unrealized gains are not taxed.

What is the difference in tax rates between ordinary income and capital gains?

Capital-gains tax is what you pay on your profits when you have bought a stock (or other "capital asset") and have held it for at least 12 months and one day before selling it. This is referred to as the long-term capital-gains tax. If you do not hold your stock for at least 12 months and one day before selling it, you will owe ordinary income taxes on your gain; this is referred to as a short-term captial-gains tax.

In the two lowest income-tax brackets, the long-term capital-gains tax rate is only 5 percent. For everyone else, it is 15 percent. The tax rate on stock dividends is also 15 percent or 5 percent. (Both these rates are due to expire in 2010.) You owe ordinary income taxes on interest payments you receive. The top tax rate for ordinary income is now 35 percent.

How do I figure my annual rate of return?

The rate of return is a percentage measure of the profit on your stock from the time you bought it to the time you sold it, or until the present if you have not sold it. The annual rate of return is the percentage increase of profit for a 12-month period.

Let's say you put $25,000 into a stock. One year later, this stock is valued at $30,000. That's a $5,000 gain. Add to this figure any dividends paid to you by the stock company during that year—let's say $750. Your total gain is $5,750. Now divide that number by the amount of your original investment ($5,750 divided by $25,000). The result is 23 percent, and that is your rate of return. For an annual rate of return, follow the same process, beginning with the dollar value of your stock at the beginning of the year.

What rate of return should I expect from my stocks?

You want at least to be keeping pace with the overall return of the stock market. If you are not keeping pace, you might be better off in an index fund or with SPDRs.

FINANCIAL ADVISERS

You haven't said much about financial advisers. What's wrong with handing my money over to one of them?

Nothing, as long as you pick one who's reputable. But employing a financial adviser doesn't let you off the hook. *You* are responsible for your money.

What should I tell my financial adviser?

If you have a financial adviser, I want you to begin by telling him or her very little about how much money you have to invest and a great deal about your overall financial goals and situation, including the amount of credit card debt you have. After all, if you are going to hire someone to look after your money, invest it for you, and make sure it remains safe, that person should know everything about your financial picture, including your outstanding debts and your hopes and goals for the future.

What kinds of questions should a financial adviser be asking me?

A financial adviser should try to find out all your financial particulars in as much detail as possible. If I were your adviser, I would ask: Do you have credit card debt? Do you own a home? If not, do you want to buy a home? Do you need to buy any large-ticket items, like a car? What are your total current sources of income? What are your expenses? Do you have a retirement plan? Will you be receiving a pension? And here are two important questions: If you want to invest, how long can you let your money work for you, without touching it? What are your investment goals and dreams?

A financial adviser should also ask you about your family. Will you inherit money from older relatives someday? If an accident or illness struck a member of your family, would you be financially responsible? Next, what about your children, if you have any? Will you be paying for their college educations?

And all this is just for starters. Only after many more questions should an adviser ask how much you have to invest. If the adviser asks that question first, find the door.

Are there different kinds of financial advisers?

Yes. There are many titles and certifications for advisers. Some financial advisers are far more qualified than others. Some advisers will just provide you with a financial plan and send you home to carry it out. Others will advise you for as long as you want, taking care of your money over the long term.

What sort of education, or degrees, should a financial adviser have?

If your adviser is simply a money manager, he or she could be a financial adviser at a brokerage firm or a registered investment adviser. If you need an overall financial plan, however, your adviser should, in my opinion, be a certified financial planner professional. A certified financial planner professional has had to pass a series of exams that test his or her knowledge of every aspect of finance, including risk management, retirement planning, taxes, and estate planning. It usually takes two years to study for and pass these exams. Those who do pass are required to stay up to date by taking continuing education courses and to abide by the standards of the Certified Financial Planner Board of Standards/CFP Board.

How should I prepare for the interview? Should my partner come with me?

If you are married, or living with someone with whom you are financially bound, you should go to see the adviser together. But before you go into the office of a financial adviser, you and your partner should do your homework. Discuss what you want to accomplish with the adviser. Find out whether you agree on your financial goals and investment strategies. Talk out all your hopes and fears about money. Make sure you both have a solid understanding of where you stand financially right now. And remember, after you've chosen an adviser, you and your spouse or partner must make all decisions as a team, and must both keep up-to-date with what the adviser is doing.

Once I've retained a financial adviser, what should I expect of him or her?

Insist, first and foremost, that the adviser contact you every single time he or she makes a change in your account. Not only that, but your adviser should also explain to you in clear, simple language the reason for every transaction. I would insist that you be informed about the tax implications of a sale. Each and every commission should be explained. After each transaction, your adviser should send you a transaction slip from the brokerage firm that holds your money, telling you what has been bought or sold—and that slip should always match transactions for which you gave permission.

Will I get a monthly statement in the mail?

Yes. On that statement, you should expect to see a detailed summary of the month's transactions, including deposits, withdrawals, and current positions held. This statement must come directly from the brokerage firm that is holding your money, not from your adviser's office. Along these same lines, your financial adviser must prepare for you both quarterly reports and an annual report.

What is inside a quarterly or an annual report of my account?

In both your quarterly and your annual reports, you should find the exact return your financial adviser is getting on your money, as well as all fees and commissions he or she has charged you. (The figure on his or her report must match the report that is generated directly by the brokerage firm.) These reports should also show you all realized gains or losses (all the money you actually made or lost from selling investments) and all unrealized gains and losses (gains and losses on investments you own but have not yet sold). If mutual funds are involved, these reports should include returns of the overall index, so you know whether you're doing better or worse than the index in question.

How much of a return on my money can I rightfully expect?

The return your financial adviser makes for you after all commissions and fees should be equal to or better than the return on the Standard & Poor's 500 Index.

What should I be careful of when dealing with a financial adviser?

A bona fide financial adviser will never, ever ask you to write a check made out to him or her personally. All the money that you hand over must be placed in an institution (such as Schwab, Merrill Lynch, or Fidelity, for example), and every check you write should therefore be made payable to that institution. This is absolutely essential. More than one "adviser" has flown the coop with the money of dozens of clients. And you should never allow your financial adviser to pressure you into doing something that runs counter to what your inner voice is telling you.

FEE-BASED ADVISERS

How do financial advisers charge for their services?

There are a few different ways. For example, some financial advisers will offer you a free consultation—a kind of meet-and-greet. An adviser who sees you for free is trying to convince you to allow him or her to invest your money for you, so that he or she can reap the commissions.

I went for a free consultation and wrote a check to buy a mutual fund. Did that include a commission for the financial adviser as well?

You betcha. If you go to see an adviser for free, so to speak, and hand over $40,000 to him or her to invest in a loaded mutual fund (a mutual fund with sales charges), then in fact you will have just paid about 5 percent, or $2,000, for that so-called "free" session. The moment you sit down in that office and tell a commission-based adviser how much money you have to invest, he or she knows exactly what it means for him or her. If you come in with $100,000, your adviser can make about $5,000—not bad for an hour or two of work!

What is a fee-based financial adviser?

A fee-based adviser is one who charges you an hourly fee to tell you what to do with your money. He or she does not actually invest the money for you. You leave the office in possession of what you have to assume is good advice, and then you make the various transactions yourself.

What about a fees-plus-commissions arrangement?

Here, you pay the financial adviser in two tiers: You pay him or her a fee to tell you what to do and, for that fee, the adviser will create a master plan for you. If you decide you want him or her to do the actual investing for you—which many people do—the adviser will receive commissions on the transactions.

REGISTERED INVESTMENT ADVISERS

What is a registered investment adviser?

A registered investment adviser (RIA) is a person who manages your money for you by buying and selling most types of investments on your behalf. Such an adviser makes all the decisions about your investment account. RIAs usually require a fairly large minimum initial investment, ranging from $50,000 to $5 million. The average minimum is between $150,000 and $250,000.

How do RIAs make their money?

An RIA manages your money on an ongoing basis, for a fee that is usually a percentage of the money under management. This percentage can range from 0.25 to 3 percent a year, but I believe you should not pay more than 1.5 percent, including all commissions.

Think about this fee structure for a moment. The amount you pay your RIA is a percentage of the money he or she is managing: Isn't this a terrific incentive for him or her to make your money grow? Suppose you gave your RIA $100,000 to invest and agreed to pay a 1 percent management fee. The RIA knows that if the account stays at $100,000 over the next year, he or she will make $1,000 in management fees. If the account doubles, he or she will make $2,000. But if the account is worth only $50,000 at the end of the year, your RIA will make only $500. If you make money, your RIA makes money. If you lose money, so does your RIA.

You seem to think highly of RIAs.

In many situations, I do, because an RIA is on your team, in downtimes and uptimes.

But isn't it dangerous to give someone else so much control over my money?

Good question. If you hire an RIA, please make sure that your assets are held in a reputable institution, such as Charles Schwab or Fidelity, and that all the RIA has the right to do is buy or sell on your behalf—not to withdraw money, except for any predetermined fees he or she is owed. And even though you are granting your RIA permission to trade your account without notifying you each and every time, it is still your responsibility to keep yourself informed about what securities and assets you own and what they are earning. And make sure you can termi-

nate your agreement at any time if you don't like the performance of your RIA (whether or not there are fees for doing so).

BROKERAGE FIRMS:
FULL SERVICE OR DISCOUNT?

**_What is the difference between a full-service broker
and a discount broker?_**
Basically, the difference is the amount of money you pay the
broker to hold your hand and your money. A full-service brokerage firm offers its customers just about every financial service you can think of—research reports, professional advice,
and even tax preparation. But in return for all these services
(and the overhead, which can be fairly high), you must pay
high commissions. A discount brokerage firm eliminates all
the extras in exchange for a significant reduction in fees. In my
opinion, with the evolution of the Internet and all the
resources that are now available to you, you can have access to
all the vital information you need and still take advantage of
the low costs of a discount broker.

**_Is there any way I can get a discount on the commis-
sion I pay my full-service broker?_**
If you do a lot of trading, it doesn't hurt to try. If your account
is a good one, your broker may be glad to adjust the scale of
his or her commissions. After all, this is a competitive profes-
sion, and your broker knows that there are discount brokerages
out there that could do what he or she does for a lot less.

**_I have just inherited a lot of money and feel as if I
want to use a full-service broker, but everyone is telling_**

me that's an old-fashioned idea. What do you think?
I think that you are not alone. It seems to me that the more money people have, the more they tend to use a full-service broker. There's nothing wrong with this, per se. The real question is which full-service broker you should choose, for they are not created equal.

If you go the full-service route, be sure all your needs are going to be met, since you'll be paying for it. You also may want to check out an RIA.

When considering a full-service brokerage firm, what questions should I ask?

Here are the areas of importance to investigate:

1. How much does the broker charge to invest your money—for wrap accounts, commissions, and fee-based accounts attached to asset size?
2. Does the brokerage firm have a solid research department with a good track record in the stocks it recommends?
3. Does the brokerage firm monitor its brokers? Ask to see the conduct record of its brokers to see whether they tend to get into trouble or are honest.
4. Does the brokerage firm provide the services that you want in person and online?
5. Are the brokerage firm's statements easy to understand? Ask to see a sample statement. If you cannot understand it, chances are it will be hard for you to tell whether your adviser is doing a good job or not.

Which full-service brokers are rated most highly?

A 2006 *Smart Money* magazine survey ranked the top seven full-service brokerage firms. Merrill Lynch was the overall winner. Next was Smith Barney, and in third place was Edward Jones. The firms at the bottom of the list were A. G. Edwards, Wachovia, Morgan Stanley, and UBS. But check each firm thoroughly; these things keep changing.

Smart Money's survey also ranked the brokerages by categories. For customer satisfaction, Edward Jones came in first, A. G. Edwards came in second, and in third place was Wachovia.

For stock picking, Wachovia placed first, A. G. Edwards, Merrill Lynch, and UBS tied for second place, with four stars each.

For statements, Edward Jones was the winner, Merrill Lynch second, and Morgan Stanley third.

On the issue of trust, Edward Jones came in first, A. G. Edwards second, and Wachovia third.

All these factors should be considered when choosing a broker, because it is not enough to get full service—you also want good service.

When I hear the term "discount brokerage," I think it sounds unsafe. Am I right?

Not at all. Paying less money doesn't necessarily mean you get less quality. The word "discount" here refers to the huge savings you can reap simply because discount brokerage firms do not perform the full array of services that full-service brokerage firms do. You can save up to 90 percent on commissions if you trade through a discount brokerage firm!

What don't discount brokerage firms provide me?

Typically, they will not give you any investment advice, such as when to buy or sell a particular stock. Good advice is one of those things that brokerage firms overprice, and that takes a giant bite out of your wallet. Knowing about stocks and what you want from them is up to you. I would recommend using a discount broker only when you feel confident enough to make your own decisions regarding stocks.

Can I get research reports from a discount brokerage firm?

In most cases, yes, though sometimes for a fee. At some firms, such as Fidelity and Schwab, these research reports will contain recommendations and opinions from experienced analysts. But once you're finished reading these reports, it's up to you to make the decision to invest or not.

Do discount brokers keep regular nine-to-five hours?

You can contact most discount brokerage firms 24 hours a day, every day, because these companies offer automated service lines. These days, a lot of discount brokerage firms also allow customers to monitor their investments online, via the firm's Web page.

Do you recommend using a discount broker?

Again, I recommend using a discount broker when you are sure that you know the ropes of investing. Why pay a full commission if you don't have to? Once you have the know-how and the experience to manage your investments without the advice of a professional, I think discount brokerage firms are the way to go.

What about using a broker at my bank?

I would strongly advise against using a broker at your bank. Most of these people have very little true brokerage experience, and they seldom stay in the position of broker for very long. They usually can sell you only loaded mutual funds.

INVESTING ONLINE

I have a friend who says he makes all his trades online. Do you recommend it?

As with using a discount broker, it's important to make absolutely sure that you thoroughly understand how to invest, the risks involved, and what kind of an investor you are before you invest online. Your goals should be clear-cut, and the amount of time you have to let your money grow should also be well defined. You should have called the companies in which you are interested in investing and requested as much information from them as they were willing to send you. In short, if you have done your homework and if you are reasonably confident about the decisions you're making, then investing online is the way to go.

Is giving out information about myself online, including the securities I'm investing in, safe?

In the past, I've been very wary of providing information such as credit card numbers over the World Wide Web, but much has been made of the high-security developments in encryption software used by most reputable online vendors. Many analysts involved in online brokerage firms swear that there is next to no risk in providing the firm with certain sensitive information, including how much money you have to invest and which securities you're investing in. Online firms generally offer top-notch security, though you might want to make sure that the online brokerage you choose offers SSL encryption services, which disguise the data you provide them with a sophisticated code. Still, I would advise you to give out only the minimum information required by the brokerage firm. Skip any listings with the word "optional" after them.

How do online brokerage firms charge for their services?

Many online brokerages charge different amounts for different kinds of trades. As always, read the fine print. Do you want to make a market order? This will cost you, say, $8. What about a limit order? This could cost you $12. And just as with an offline brokerage firm, there may be other hidden fees that you should know about before you commit to anything.

Do Internet brokerage firms' chat rooms—or any Internet chat rooms—have valuable information that I should be aware of?

Chat rooms are just that—chat rooms, forums in which people like you from across the country, and sometimes around the world, offer their opinions. Take whatever you hear in Web chat rooms with a grain of salt—even what you hear in chat rooms that are connected to an online brokerage firm's homepage.

If I open an account with an online brokerage firm, will I be able to access my account whenever I want?

You can access most online—and even traditional—brokerage accounts 24 hours a day, though there may be some restrictions. Check with the firm you are considering for its particular rules.

What if I need to talk to a living, breathing human being and not a computer screen?

Again, an investor's access to a customer service representative varies from firm to firm. Check with the online firm in question.

Is it possible to get advice from an actual broker within an online brokerage firm?

In many cases, it is, though you will often have to pay for this service. Some online brokerage firms offer financial advice, portfolio tips, and even the results of their research to investors, but first you should find out how much, if anything, this will cost you.

How do I go about choosing an online brokerage firm?

First of all, ask yourself what you want out of it. Are you a fanatic buyer and seller? In that case, you would need constant access to the firm for those middle-of-the-night trades. Are you looking for a firm that trades not just in stocks and bonds but also in mutual funds, and that can even arrange to pay your bills every month? Then you would probably be in search of an online brokerage firm that offers its customers a full menu of services.

What other questions should I ask an online brokerage firm?

After you've found out what products the online brokerage firm offers—mutual funds? money-market accounts? company analysis?—you should find out the firm's hours of operation. Are customer service representatives on call throughout the day? From nine to five? Or not at all? Is the firm registered with the Securities and Exchange Commission? (You can access the SEC's website at *www.sec.gov* to find out if a firm is registered and also whether any complaints have been lodged against the firm. The firm you choose should be registered with the SEC.)

Here are some more questions to ask:

1. What is the fee schedule?
2. How much money does it take to open an account? (Most online brokerage firms require an initial investment of at least $2,000.)
3. If your balance falls below a certain amount, are any penalties assessed?

4. Does the firm offer stock quotes? Are they quoted in real time, or an hour behind? If the firm offers real-time quotes, is this service free or will they charge you a little extra for the privilege of watching your stock prices fluctuate?

5. Ask to see a sample statement. Can you understand it easily?

6. What does the online firm charge to trade on margin?

7. Is the firm responsive to your calls?

8. Does the firm's website go down very often? (If everyone is trying to trade at once and the site goes down, you could lose a lot of money. This happens more often than you may think.)

9. Finally, I'd ask myself, is the site easily accessible? And is it easy to navigate?

Should I choose an online broker on the basis of how much it charges to make a trade?

No. Please choose an online broker based on its ability to get you the best execution, or per-share price, at the time you make a trade. With slow or sloppy execution, you could lose a lot more money than you can save with bargain-priced trading charges. For example, let's say you buy 1,000 shares of a stock selling at $35. With slow execution, you might pay $35.25 for the stock instead of $35. At that price your shares would cost you a total of $35,250 instead of $35,000. I'd rather pay a $25 trading charge than an $8 charge plus $250 in a higher per-share price.

In Your Interest

Bonds fall into the category of debt investments, and most people buy them for the income they produce. They are issued by a corporation, a municipality, the U.S. government, or an agency of the government that is in need of money and is willing to go into debt and borrow that money to meet its needs. When you buy a bond, you are the lender, and the issuer of the bond is the debtor.

Every long-term investor comes to the bond market eventually, but to many people bonds are even less familiar than stocks. Bonds don't usually make headlines; they're not exciting, but the fact that they're unexciting, of course, is precisely the point. So read on.

Bond Basics

What is a bond?
A bond is a debt security, or IOU, issued by a corporation or government agency in exchange for the money you lend it. In most instances, bond issuers agree to repay their loans by a specific date—and to make regular interest payments to you until that date. The interest rate, called a "coupon," does not change. That's why bonds are often referred to as "fixed-income" investments. The end date that the issuer has to pay you your principal is called the maturity date.

How far into the future can a maturity date go?
Anywhere from one to 100 years, but the usual repayment period of a long-term bond is not more than 30 years.

Why do you call the interest rate of a bond a "coupon"?
Before securities were traded electronically, buyers actually received engraved bonds from the issuer. You kept them as if they were cash, in the bank or some other safe place, because they were as good as cash. Your name as the owner was not printed on them. In order to get your interest payments, you had to physically clip one of the coupons attached to the bond and give it to the bank, which would hand you the money. Ditto for when you wanted your investment money back at maturity. This system was a blessing for crooks, but everyone else found it a nuisance, and by the early 1980s the technology was in place to toss the so-called "coupon clippers" into history's wastebasket. We're still left with "coupon," though, as a synonym for the interest figure that was printed on the bond.

When do I get my interest payments?
Most bonds pay interest semiannually, calculated backward from the month on which the bond is due to mature. So if you bought a $10,000 bond with a maturity date of June 2014 and an interest rate, or coupon, of 6 percent, your interest payments would total $600 a year. You would get $300 in June and $300 in December.

When do I get my original investment back?
With most bonds, the issuer must give you your investment money back, at face value, on the maturity date of the bond—June 2014, in our example.

What does a bond cost to buy, and what is the face value of a bond?
What a bond costs depends on when you buy it and from whom you buy it. Did you buy it from the issuer—that is, in the primary market? Or did you buy it secondhand, so to

speak? Most "new" bonds are issued at what's called "par." For corporate bonds, par value is normally $1,000; for government bonds it can be much higher. If you buy a bond when it is issued, you usually pay par for it. Then, when the bond matures, you get back the par price, or face value, of the bond. The secondary market becomes important when you want to sell a bond before its maturity date, but in that market you may get par, more than par, or less than par for your bond, depending on the demand among other investors.

OK, but why would anyone want to sell a "fixed-income" bond before its maturity date?

There's a market for everything, as you know, and there's one for "used" bonds. Investors might want to sell bonds before their maturity date because they need the money, or because the price other investors are willing to pay for the bond has gone up, or perhaps because the price has gone down and they want to sell the bond at a loss and deduct the loss from their taxes.

This leads to an important point: Although you pay regular income taxes on the interest payments from many bonds, you can also generate capital gains (taxed at a rate lower than ordinary income) by selling your bond at a profit on the secondary market, if you've owned it for at least a year. Conversely, if you sell a bond for less than you paid for it, you may incur a capital loss that you can deduct from your income taxes.

What makes a bond's price go up and down? I thought a bond was a fixed income investment, meaning nothing about it changes.

Even though a bond's interest rate and maturity date are fixed, the price at which you can sell a bond on the secondary market, before its maturity date, is not fixed. That's because the economic environment in which bonds are bought and sold is never fixed. In particular, as the Federal Reserve Bank tries to dampen inflation or spur growth by changing federal interest rates, the demand for bonds—and their selling price—goes up or down.

Imagine, for example, that you bought $10,000 worth of a ten-year bond that pays a 6 percent coupon. Now, suddenly, the Fed raises interest rates to 8 percent. Understandably, you might want to sell your bond and buy one with the higher interest rate. Trouble is, who in their right mind would want to buy your bond at the price you paid for it—par, or $10,000?—when the coupon is only 6 percent? No one, since anyone who wants a bond can go out and buy a new one and get an 8 percent coupon. So, in order to sell your bond, you would have to lower the price. Think about it. If the selling price for your bond were lowered to about $8,000 and the person who bought your bond would be getting $600 a year (6 percent of the $10,000 face value of the bond), then, at the $8,000 price, the bond's yield would rise to 7.5 percent. Someone might think about buying it at that price—especially because, when the bond matures, it will pay him or her the face value, or $10,000. So not only would the buyer be getting a good current yield, but his yield to maturity would be so good that it would make this bond competitive with the new bonds paying higher interest rates.

So I can sell a bond at any time from the moment I purchase it from the issuer to the moment of its maturity? That's right. Depending on what is happening in the Fed-controlled interest-rate environment, the price of a bond on the secondary market may go above or below par. The dynamic is quite simple once you get the hang of it. When general interest rates go up, the current price of bonds goes down. And when general interest rates go down, the current price of bonds goes up. If you pay above par, you've bought at what's called a premium. If you pay below par, you've bought at a discount.

What does the term "current yield" mean?

It's a very important concept! The current yield is the real interest rate of a bond, based on what you paid for it. Let's go back to that 6 percent $10,000 bond that you bought from the issuer. At the moment you bought it, your current yield was just what the coupon said—6 percent, or $600 a year. Since then, however, the interest-rate environment has changed, downward this time, with the result that your bond is now selling on the secondary market for more than you paid for it— say, about $11,000. You decide to sell. But the would-be buyer, if he's experienced, must now calculate his current yield before going on to purchase the bond for $11,000. The bond will always have a fixed coupon of 6 percent, or $600 a year, but since the buyer will be paying $11,000 for that yield, his current yield is really only 5.45 percent. In the secondary market, current yield is what a bond purchased on the secondary market will really yield, right now, once the price paid on the secondary market is taken into account. Never buy a bond from anyone other than the issuer without first calculating the current yield. Then, still before you buy, calculate the yield to maturity.

What is "yield to maturity"?

Yield to maturity is the actual percentage return you will make on your money at the end of the bond's life. It includes not only the coupon yield—in our example, $600 a year—and the $10,000 par value you get back at maturity, but also the discount or premium you paid for the bond on the secondary market. If you bought the bond from the issuer and you kept it to maturity, your current yield and the yield to maturity would both be 6 percent. But if you bought a 10-year bond, for example, two years after it was issued, and paid $11,000 for it, then you would have to figure in an overpayment of $1,000 when calculating your yield to maturity. Why? Because when the bond matures you will get $10,000, and that is a loss of $1,000, given what you paid for the bond. The current yield in this case would be 5.45 percent, but the yield to maturity, including that $1,000 loss, would be 4.5 percent. Basically, with yield to maturity, you have to spread your $1,000 loss over eight years of collecting interest on the bond. On the other hand, if you bought the bond for $8,000 two years after it was issued and it matured eight years later at $10,000, your current yield would be 7.5 percent, but your yield to maturity would be 9.7 percent. In this case, you are spreading out a $2,000 gain. That is, unless your bond has a call feature.

What is a "call feature"?

Most issuers of bonds protect themselves with a call feature against paying more interest than the current market demands. A call feature allows the issuer to give you your money back before the maturity date of the bond or, in the language of bonds, to "call in" the bond. The call feature tells you at what point the bond can be called in, as well as how much the issuer has to pay you if it does call in the bond.

Under what circumstance would an issuer call in a bond before its maturity date?

An issuer might call in a bond if interest rates come down after the bond has been issued. The issuer can then pay off all the investors and issue a new bond at a lower interest rate. But the call feature is not such a good thing for the investor. Let's say you bought a $1,000 30-year bond that was issued in 1989 with a coupon of 9 percent. And let's say that this bond had a call feature specifying that after the year 2000 the bond could be called in at a price of $1,020 a bond. Remember that you paid par, or $1,000, for the bond when you bought it. The issuer could take the bond back by paying you a mere $20 premium. Now that may not seem like such a bad deal, but what if current interest rates are only at 7 percent when this happens? If you still need income, you will only be able to invest this money at 7 percent, instead of the 9 percent you were getting.

Beware of call features when you buy a bond. You do not want to have to give up a good interest rate without your consent. Corporate and municipal bonds can have a call feature; Treasuries seldom do. (The exceptions are Treasuries issued before 1985.) Government agency bonds (such as Ginnie Maes and Freddie Macs) are all callable.

Purchasing Bonds

How can I buy a bond?

The most common way to buy bonds is to open an account with a broker and place your order. You can use either a full-service broker or a discount broker to execute your trades. EE/I bonds and Treasury securities can also be purchased directly from the U.S. Treasury Department by establishing an account with TreasuryDirect. For more information, visit the TreasuryDirect website, *www.treasurydirect.gov.*

How much do brokers charge in commissions?

Watch out! Bond brokers are tricky when it comes to their commissions. They usually build them into the price of the bond. Moreover, commissions vary widely from brokerage firm to brokerage firm. Thus, the same bond can give you a different return on your investment, depending on where you buy it. Be sure to shop around.

Do all bonds trade on the secondary bond market as easily as stocks trade on the stock market?

Like some stocks, some bonds aren't readily sold, or "liquid." Others, like Treasuries, sell in huge numbers all the time. Make sure the bonds that you are considering are quality bonds that can be easily sold. (I'll say more about this later.)

How are bond prices listed?

The price of a bond is always quoted in hundreds—not in thousands—of its par value. In the newspaper and on your monthly statement, a bond will be valued at $100, for instance, which seems puzzling. But just add a zero to the number, and you will get the true figure—$1,000.

BOND RATINGS

What's the best way to gauge the quality of a bond?

The best way is by consulting the rating on your bond by the two major independent rating services, Standard & Poor's and Moody's. The agencies rate bonds for safety—that is, the trustworthiness of the issuer to deliver on his IOU. Here's how each agency rates bonds, from the highest quality to the lowest:

- Standard & Poor's: AAA, AA+, AA, AA-, A+, A, A-, BBB+, BBB, BBB-, BB+, BB, BB-, B+, B, B-, CCC, and D.
- Moody's: Aaa, Aa1, Aa2, Aa3, A1, A2, A3, Baa1, Baa2, Baa3, Ba1, Ba2, Ba3, B1, B2, B3, Caa, Ca, and C.

For safety, you should consider only bonds that have a rating in the A categories; otherwise, even though you might find a higher interest rate, you could be risking your principal.

INTEREST RATES AND BONDS

Why do different bonds offer different interest rates?
The interest rate offered by a company or government agency on its bonds depends on several things: the interest rate environment at the time of issue, the issuer's reputation for safety (the interest rate must be higher if there's any risk that the issuer won't pay you back), and the length of maturity of the bond. The bottom line here is that issuers are competing to borrow your money. They know that lenders—that's you—want to get the highest interest rate available, or one that's at least competitive with other comparable rates on offer. If you could get 7 percent on a safe bond with one issuer, why on earth would you buy a bond from an identically safe issuer at 6 percent?

How does the maturity date affect the interest rate?
Theoretically, the longer an issuer asks you to tie up your money, the more the issuer should be willing to pay. After all, the issuer is asking you to take the risk that interest rates may rise between the time you buy the bond and the time it reaches maturity, and so you may potentially lose out on higher rates. However, this is not always the way things work. If a bond is issued at a time when interest rates are higher and are projected to go down, the issuer may offer higher rates for shorter maturities than for longer maturities. Therefore, it's very important to check the coupon of bonds offered at different maturities, for it may not pay you to commit your money for longer periods of time. For instance, if a 10-year bond is paying 5 percent and a 30-year bond is paying 5.1 percent, it's probably not worth tying up your money for 30 years unless

you really believe that interest rates are going to be considerably lower than 5 percent in 10 years.

Can you go back over how the overall interest rate environment affects bonds?

Just remember the cardinal rule of investing in bonds. As interest rates go up, bond prices go down on the secondary market, and as interest rates go down, bond prices go up on the secondary market. It's as simple as that.

Reality, of course, sometimes puts a wrench into the works. A bond's price does vary with changes in overall interest rates. But a bond's price on the secondary market is also influenced by the quality of the bond, the coupon, and the years remaining until it matures. The further away the maturity date and the lower the quality of the bond, the more volatile the price of a bond will be—in other words, the more it will move up or down as interest rates change. The closer the maturity date and the higher the quality of the bond, the less movement in price there will be as interest rates change.

THE RISKS OF BOND OWNERSHIP

I was told that owning a bond was safe, safe, safe, but surely there are risks?

Yes, there are no fewer than six kinds of risk—risks people usually do not think of when buying a bond. They are interest-rate risk, call risk, credit risk, inflation risk, event risk, and reinvestment risk.

What is interest-rate risk?

Interest-rate risk takes into account the fact that the market value of your bonds could fall due to rising interest rates. In general, as we've seen, bond prices decline when interest rates rise—and rise when interest rates fall.

What is call risk?

Call risk is the risk that the issuer of your bond could call, or prepay, it. During periods of declining interest rates, corporate and municipal bond issuers prefer to prepay their loans before maturity and reissue the loans at a lower interest rate. You, as lender, then must reinvest your principal earlier than you had expected—and probably also at a lower interest rate.

What is credit risk?

Credit risk is a gamble on the creditworthiness of the issuer. If a bond issuer defaults—that is, fails to make timely payments of principal and interest—or if a bond's credit rating is reduced, thereby reducing its resale value, you could lose money.

What is inflation risk?

Inflation, a rise in the price of the goods and services we all consume, is a general risk of financial life. It can erode the value of your paycheck, of your stocks, and especially of your bonds. Before buying a bond, please take into account any signs of increasing inflation. Among other things, inflation can make your fixed interest rate less valuable and can mean a rise in overall interest rates above the rates on the bond you're considering buying.

What is event risk?

Event risk refers to the possibility that the company or agency that issued your bond will undergo a change and that the credit quality or market value of your bonds could suffer in response to an event such as a merger, a leveraged buyout, or other corporate restructuring.

What is reinvestment risk?

That's just another name for the risks you run from changes in the economic environment that cut into the yield of any new investment you are forced to make.

LADDERING BONDS

I can see that time is a huge factor in the bond market, so it might make sense to buy bonds with different maturity dates. Is that right?

That is exactly right. Buying bonds with different maturity dates is a time-tested technique called "laddering." Here's why it's a good idea. Let's say you have $100,000 to invest in bonds and you want to generate income. Instead of taking the entire $100,000 and buying bonds that mature at the same time— for example, in five years—you might put $20,000 each into bonds that mature in one, two, three, four, and five years. This way, you would have $20,000 coming due to you every year for the next five years. If interest rates went up, you would simply replace the maturing bond with another bond at a higher interest rate. If interest rates remained the same, you would have lost nothing. If interest rates went down, well, you would still have some of your money invested for the next few years in bonds at the higher rate.

But suppose bonds are selling with high interest rates at the time I buy?

When interest rates are high and are expected to fall (as in the early 1980s), it is best to buy bonds with long maturities (10 to 30 years) and not to ladder them. If you had bought 30-year Treasury bonds in the 1980s, you could still be getting 15 percent a year today.

TYPES OF BONDS

The bonds that you will most commonly come into contact with on the road to wealth are government-issued bonds such as Treasury bonds, savings bonds, and municipal bonds; U.S. mortgage-backed securities such as Ginnie Maes, Fannie Maes, and Freddie Macs; corporate bonds and convertible bonds; and zero coupon bonds.

TREASURIES

What is a Treasury bond?
A Treasury bond is a bond issued by the U.S. government. Income from Treasuries is exempt from taxes at the state and local level. This is important to keep in mind, because a Treasury paying 6 percent will give you more income after taxes than a CD paying 6 percent if you live in a state and/or city that imposes income taxes. Income from Treasuries is taxed by the federal government, however.

What is the yield on Treasury bonds?
The yield on Treasuries is usually the lowest of all bonds with comparable maturities. That's the price you pay for Treasuries' unequaled safety. Treasuries are 100 percent guaranteed by the U.S. government. Only a government can make that guarantee, of course, because only a government can print more

money or raise taxes, or both, in the event that it has trouble meeting its obligations. But for this kind of security, you get a slightly lower coupon.

Do all Treasuries have the same maturity?

No. In fact, Treasuries of different maturities are known by different names:

A Treasury bill (T-bill) is usually 90 days to 12 months to maturity.

A Treasury note is usually 1 to 10 years to maturity.

A Treasury bond is usually 10 to 30 years to maturity.

Do Treasury bills pay interest?

Strictly speaking, no. Because they have such short maturities (one year and under), Treasury bills do not make interest payments before maturity. Instead, they are priced at a discount and mature at par. The difference between what you pay for the bill and what you get for it at maturity (par)—or what you get for it if you sell it prior to maturity—is the interest earned on the bill. For example, when you buy a Treasury bill, it might cost you $4,800; when it matures nine months later, you might get back $5,000. That extra $200 is your interest.

I suppose I owe federal taxes on that interest, but when do I pay it? In the year I bought the T-bill or in the year in which it matures?

With a T-bill, the year in which you receive back your investment plus interest is the year for which you owe taxes on any earnings. If you bought a T-bill in 2006 and it matures in 2007, you won't owe taxes on your interest until 2007. When people buy large numbers of Treasury bills, they should take tax vulnerability at the time of maturity into account.

What are TIPS?

TIPS are Treasury Inflation-Indexed Securities also sometimes referred to as Treasury Inflation-Protected Securities. TIPS are considered to be the safest type of investment because their ultimate value cannot be diminished by inflation. Since the principal value of these securities is tied to inflation, TIPS are protected against inflation. TIPS are similar to other notes and bonds in that you receive interest payments every six months and a payment of principal when the security matures. But with TIPS the interest and redemption payments are tied to inflation. Unlike other marketable Treasury securities, TIPS can't be reinvested. Similar to other Treasury notes and bonds, TIPS are exempt from state and local income taxes, and subject to federal income tax. In regards to federal taxes, there is one issue to be aware of: In any year when the principal of your TIPS increases, that gain is reportable income for that year, even though you won't receive your inflation-adjusted principal until the security matures.

Do Treasury notes and bonds pay interest?

Yes. Every six months you will receive your interest payments. Federal taxes will be due when you file that year's tax return.

Where is the best place to buy Treasuries?

The best way to buy a Treasury that's just been issued by the government is through what's known as a TreasuryDirect account, which you can set up directly with the U.S. Treasury Department. You can also buy a Treasury through a broker, but the broker—unlike TreasuryDirect—will charge you a fee.

Will a TreasuryDirect account do anything else besides provide me access to commission-free Treasuries?

Yes. A TreasuryDirect account will hold your TIPS, T-bills, T-notes, and T-bonds, and any interest you earn on these can be electronically deposited in the account. You will receive a statement when your Treasuries are issued, reinvested, or redeemed, or when any other changes are made to your account. Or, if you have a brokerage or money-market account, automatic payments of interest and principal can be made electronically to that account. Contact Treasury-Direct on the World Wide Web at *www.treasurydirectl.gov/,* or call (800) 722-2678.

SAVINGS BONDS

What is a savings bond?

A savings bond is another type of bond issued by the U.S. government. You can buy savings bonds in face values ranging from $50 to $10,000. One great advantage of these bonds is that they come in so many denominations. (Another advantage is that, like all federal bonds, they pay interest that is exempt from state and local taxes, though not from federal taxes.) Many people have received savings bonds as gifts from parents or grandparents, have bought them as savings vehicles for themselves, or have given them to children. The problem is that there's a tendency to put them away and never look at them again. This is a big mistake. After their maturity and an extension period (please see the following questions), savings bonds, like other bonds, stop earning interest. Over a longer period of time, even a low rate of inflation can seriously erode their face value. If you buy or own savings bonds, please remember to redeem them when they have reached their full maturity and/or after you've reached the end of your extensions. There are two kinds of savings bonds currently being issued, known as series EE/E and I bonds. (Series E bonds, the predecessor to EE bonds, are no longer issued by the U.S.

Treasury, nor are Series HH/H bonds, though many people still hold them.)

What is a series EE/E savings bond?

A series EE/E bond is a savings bond that you purchase at a 50 percent discount from face value. When you buy a $100 EE/E bond, for example, you pay only 50 percent of that amount, or $50. As with Treasury bills, the interest on the bond is not paid out to you; it goes back into the bond until (or sometimes even after) the bond has reached its face value, in this case $100. At that point, the bond has matured. An EE/E bond these days pays a fixed rate of interest.

How is interest calculated on a series EE/E bond?

That depends on the date of the bond. If you had bought your bond before 1995, you would have been guaranteed a mini-mum rate of interest—for example, 4 percent—or a variable, or market, rate, whichever was greater. If you bought your bond after May 1995 through April 2005, your bond earns a variable, or market, rate, based on market yields of U.S. Treasury securities. With a variable rate, the amount of time it takes to reach face value varies, too—it may happen quickly or slowly, depending on how high or low market interest rates are during the period you hold your bond. You can find details on how interest is calculated for bonds issued in these years at *www.treasurydirect.gov*. Bonds purchased after April 2005 pay a fixed rate of interest. If you decide to redeem an EE/E bond before it reaches face value, please call the Treasury department to find out the current yield—that is, what dollar amount you'll get if you redeem the bond right now. If you redeem EE/E bonds in the first five years, you'll forfeit the three most recent months' interest. After five years, there is no penalty.

The interest on an EE/E series bond compounds twice a year (when new rates are announced, on May 1 and November

THE FINAL MATURITY OF SAVINGS BONDS,
BASED ON ISSUE DATE

ORIGINAL ISSUE EE/E BOND	FINAL MATURITY, IN YEARS	FINAL MATURITY DATE
1965 or earlier	40	2005 or earlier
01/80–10/80	30	01/2010–10/2010
11/80–04/81	30	11/2010–04/2011
05/81–10/82	30	05/2011–10/2012
11/82–10/86	30	11/2012–10/2016
11/86–02/93	30	11/2016–02/2023
03/93–04/95	30	03/2023–04/2025
05/95–present	30	05/2025–

1 of every year), but interest is "paid" only when the bond is redeemed. As you have seen, you can redeem your bond at any time before maturity, at maturity, or even after maturity (during one or more extension periods that prolong your interest payments after the bond has reached face value). If you hold your bond long enough, its redemption value will eventually exceed its face value.

How do I find out when my EE/E bonds mature?
First, let me explain a little more about how EE/E bonds "mature." "Original maturity" is the term used for the date when an EE/E bond achieves its face value. Bond owners often mistakenly assume that EE/E bonds stop earning interest when they reach their face value, but they don't. They go on earning interest until what's called "final maturity."

Basically, with an EE/E bond, face value isn't crucial. Final maturity is what's really important. This is the point at which your extension periods run out and beyond which your bond will no longer earn any interest nor increase in face value. The final maturity on all EE/E savings bonds issued after 1965 is 30 years from the date of original issue. Check your savings bond inventory from time to time and promptly cash in or exchange all bonds that are no longer earning interest. If you don't redeem bonds that have reached their final maturity, you will be lending the U.S. government money free of charge.

Find the issue date on your series EE/E bond and match it to the issue date in the table on page 106, and you'll find your bond's final maturity.

What happens after a bond reaches its "original" maturity date?

It sounds complicated, but it really isn't. The original maturity date is simply the date when the bond achieves its face value. At this point, without your doing anything at all, the bond will enter what is known as an extension period. The extension period can last as long as the difference between your original issue date and 30 years from that issue date. During the extension period, your bond will continue to earn interest; in other words, it will keep accumulating value—but not forever.

After 30 years is when the trouble can begin. At final maturity, bonds stop earning interest, though you can still redeem them. So if you or your parents have some bonds hidden away, please go find them and check their final maturities.

What if the bonds I have in my desk drawer haven't reached final maturity?

They'll still be earning interest. During their extension, Series EE/E or savings bonds issued at the dates below earn these guaranteed minimum yield rates:

11/82–10/86	7.5 percent
11/86–2/93	6 percent

| 03/93–4/95 | 4 percent |
| 05/95–present | There is no guaranteed minimum yield for bonds entering an extension during this period. |

How can I calculate my interest?

The Savings Bond Earnings Report—online at *www.treasury direct.gov/indiv/tools/tools_earningsreports.htm*, or call (800) 553-2663—will tell you what your bond is currently earning and will give you the current value of $100 EE/E bonds. If you don't happen to have $100 bonds, you can calculate the value of your bonds by multiplying or dividing by the appropriate number. For example, if you have a $50 bond, just divide the current value of the $100 bond by 2. If you have a $500 bond, multiply the value of the $100 bond by 5.

How and when do I redeem my EE/E savings bonds?

You can redeem your bonds at any time, but be prepared for a significant tax hit if you have not been reporting your interest payments on you tax returns. The bonds are exempt from state and local taxes, but not federal taxes. Before 2004 you could spread out the tax bite by exchanging your matured bonds for HH/H bonds—whose interest must be reported annually—but that option is no longer available.

Is a series EE/E bond a good vehicle for saving for college?

Yes, it can be. If you redeem an EE/E bond to pay for a child's qualified education expenses, you may not owe any federal taxes on the interest—that is, if your income is not too high for you to qualify. (In 2006, the income limits on using tax-advantaged EE/E bonds to pay for your child's education were as follows: For single taxpayers, the tax exclusion began to be reduced with a $63,100 modified adjusted gross income and was eliminated for adjusted gross incomes of $78,100 and above in the year the educational expenses were paid. For married taxpayers filing jointly, the tax exclusion began to be reduced with a $94,700 modified adjusted gross income and was eliminated for adjusted gross incomes of $124,700 and above in the year the educational expenses were paid.) Consult a tax preparer to discuss your situation.

In what denominations are series EE/E savings bonds available?

They're available in denominations of $50, $75, $100, $200, $500, $1,000, $5,000, and $10,000. The maximum dollar amount of series EE/E bonds you can buy in any one year is $30,000 face value, for which you will pay $15,000. (There is no maximum on the HH/H series. See below.)

Tax considerations apart, do series HH/H bonds work the same way as EE/E bonds?

No. Series HH/H bonds are known as current-income securities. The HH/H bond doesn't accumulate value the way the EE/E series does. When an HH/H bond was issued, you paid the full face value ($500, $1,000, $5,000, or $10,000) and you receive interest every six months—"current income," so it's taxed on an annual basis. The interest payments on HH/H bonds can be deposited directly into any account you designate. How much interest will you earn? You learned that on the day you bought the bond, because the rate is fixed. Bonds issued January 1, 2003, through August 2004 earn 1.5 percent interest for their initial 10-year maturity period.

Though the U.S. Treasury no longer issues HH/H bonds, the HH bonds you already own are secure; you can find out more details about rates and terms at *http://www.treasurydirect .gov/indiv/products/prod_hhbonds_glance.htm.*

Here's a schedule for when HH/H bonds reach final maturity:

SERIES H

ORIGINAL ISSUE DATE	FINAL MATURITY, IN YEARS
June 1952– January 1957	29 years, 8 months
February 1957– December 1979	30 years
January 1980–August 2004 (Series HH)	20 years

What is a series I bond?

If you are looking for a place to park non–retirement account money that you want to keep safe and sound, don't need current income from, and will not need to withdraw for at least five years, you might want to look into purchasing a relatively new kind of federal savings bond called a series I bond.

Series I bonds are issued by the federal government as a protection against inflation. They have a variable interest rate, but differ from series EE/E bonds in that the I bond's interest rate changes according to rises or—theoretically—decreases in the consumer price index (a measure of inflation) rather than a change in market interest rates. If inflation goes up, so does the interest rate on these bonds. Series I bonds are available in denominations of $50, $75, $100, $200, $500, $1,000, $5,000, and $10,000. They are issued at face value, so a $500 I bond will cost you $500. You can buy a maximum of $30,000 (of face value) worth of these bonds each year. All I bonds mature in 30 years. They are exempt from state and local taxes, and you won't owe federal taxes until the bonds are redeemed.

How do series I bonds work?

The bond's inflation-adjusted interest rates are calculated twice a year by adding a fixed rate of return to the current inflation rate. An I bond issued after May 2006 earns a 1.40 percent fixed rate of return over and above the rate of inflation. In late 2006, the annualized rate of inflation as measured by the consumer price index was 3.10 percent. In other words, bonds bought from May 1, 2006, through October 31, 2006, earn 1.40 percent more than the inflation rate of 3.10 percent, for a "composite," or compound, earnings rate of 4.52 percent. The 1.40 percent portion of the rate is fixed for the life of this bond, even though the consumer price index—and your inflation adjustment—will change. New inflation adjustments are announced on May 1 and November 1 of every year. Your interest compounds semiannually and is paid when the bond is redeemed.

Why shouldn't you invest in I bonds if you need current income? Because interest on I bonds is not paid out until the bond matures or until you cash it in. Why should you use only money that you won't need for at least the next five years? Because if you come out of an I bond before five years are up, you will be charged a three-month interest penalty. If you cash in anytime after five years have passed, you can come out without any penalty at all. (However, all I bonds must be kept for a minimum of twelve months.) Finally, why are I bonds not suitable for retirement accounts? Because the interest on I bonds is tax-deferred until you withdraw the money, and at that time only federal income taxes will be owed. It makes no sense to invest retirement money in a tax-deferred account, because all retirement accounts are tax-deferred anyway. All I bonds are exempt from state income tax. I bonds can also qualify for tax-free withdrawals for certain higher-education expenses if you qualify.

How do I purchase series EE and/or series I savings bonds?

Series EE and/or series I savings bonds can be purchased through most local banks or through a payroll savings plan offered by many employers. The bank takes payment and applications for bonds and forwards them to a Federal Reserve bank, where the actual bonds are issued and mailed to the owner. The bond issue date is the date of the application, so no interest is lost. Bonds are delivered within 15 business days. You can also buy bonds online from the U.S. Treasury at *www .treasurydirect.gov.*

What is the difference between savings bonds and Treasury bonds?

Treasury bills, notes, and bonds are transferable, so that the owner of a Treasury bond can sell the bond prior to maturity, but a savings bond cannot be transferred. Savings bonds are a paper security, unlike Treasury bills, notes, and bonds, which are electronic. The minimum required to purchase Treasury bills, notes, and bonds is $1,000 (and additional amounts must be in multiples of $1,000), versus a savings bond, which you can purchase for as little as $25. Both savings bonds and Treasury bonds are issued by the Department of the Treasury.

MUNICIPAL BONDS

What is a municipal bond?

A municipal bond is a bond issued by a municipal, county, or state government agency. Generally, all municipal bonds are free of federal income taxes. If you want to avoid state income tax as well, you must purchase a municipal bond from the state in which you are currently living. Because of the tax advantage, the interest rate paid on municipal bonds is typically lower than that on other kinds of bonds. Also because of the tax advantage, they are typically held outside of retirement accounts.

How do I know if it is better for me to buy a tax-free bond, such as a municipal bond, or a taxable bond?

To figure out whether it's better for you to buy a tax-free bond or a taxable bond, divide the tax-free yield by the difference between your tax bracket and 100 percent. That will give you the equivalent taxable yield. For instance, if your tax bracket is 28 percent, and you are thinking about buying a municipal bond with a coupon, or interest rate, of 4 percent, first subtract 0.28 from 1.00, which gives you 0.72. Then divide the interest rate of the bond that you are considering, 4, by 0.72, and that will give you the equivalent taxable yield: 4 divided by 0.72 equals about 5.5 percent. If you can get a taxable bond that gives you a yield higher than the 5.5 percent you would, in effect, be getting on a municipal bond, then you should buy the taxable bond, subject to safety concerns, of course.

When do municipal bonds usually mature?

The maturity of municipal bonds ranges from five to 30 years.

Are there different kinds of municipal bonds?

Yes, there are two kinds, revenue bonds and general obligation bonds. Revenue bonds are used to finance municipal projects that generate revenue (a toll road, for example). The revenue generated by the project is then used to make interest and principal payments to the bondholders. The danger here is that if the revenues do not come in, the bondholders are at risk of losing money.

General obligation bonds are my favorite. The best ones are those backed by the "full faith and credit" of the state or local government issuing the bond and repaid out of general tax assessments by that government. If the government is solvent, this makes them safe.

How do I know if municipal bonds are right for me?

They may be right for you if you are in a high tax bracket and the yield on a municipal bond is greater than the after-tax yield on a taxable bond. If so, it makes total sense for you to consider municipals.

I remember that there was a county in southern California that defaulted on its bonds. I don't suppose there's insurance that protects you against that sort of thing?

There is such insurance, and in most cases I would suggest that you get it, especially if you are invested in a zero coupon municipal bond. If you are willing to take about a quarter of a percent less in interest on your coupon, then you can buy what is called municipal bond insurance. It guarantees that you will get back your principal, no matter what happens. Certain bonds come with this insurance, but before you buy one, please note the name of the insurer. The top three companies offering this kind of insurance are: the Municipal Bond Insurance Association (MBIA); the American Municipal Bond Assurance Corporation (AMBAC); and the Financial Security Assurance (FSA). If your broker tells you that an insurer other than one of these three is insuring the bond on offer, be wary. These three companies are the ones to trust.

U.S. MORTGAGE–BACKED BONDS

You mentioned Ginnie Maes, Fannie Maes, and Freddie Macs. How do they work?

They are bonds issued by quasi-governmental agencies, with some backing by the U.S. government. They are considered safe bonds. Ginnie Mae, for example, is an acronym for the Government National Mortgage Association. Ginnie Maes are issued to assure that there's enough money in the banking system for homeowners, especially those applying for mortgages through the Federal Housing Authority or the Department of Veterans Affairs, to tap into for mortgages. Fannie Maes are bonds issued by the Federal National Mortgage Association, and Freddie Macs are bonds of the Federal Home Loan Mortgage Corporation.

How do I know if these bonds are right for me?

Unlike Treasury bonds and notes, which make interest payments every six months, Ginnie Maes pay interest once a month. If you are looking for monthly income, Ginnie Maes may not be a bad place to start—but learn the facts first, so you won't be surprised. Ginnie Maes typically pay 0.5 to 1 percent above the rate a regular Treasury pays, and they usually have maturities of 15 to 30 years. However, payment schedules show that 80 to 90 percent of Ginnie Maes are "called"—that is, paid off—by the 12th year.

What are the drawbacks of Ginnie Maes?

The reason Ginnie Maes pay monthly is that mortgage borrowers pay monthly, and those mortgage payments are passed right on to the investor. When interest rates go down and homeowners refinance their mortgages, or pay off their loans ahead of time, then Ginnie Mae has to pass those reductions on to you. Thus, at the very time when you want to be locked into the high interest rate of your original investment, you may be getting all your money back.

Another thing to consider: Mortgage payments comprise both interest and principal. Here's how this could affect you. Let's say you bought a Ginnie Mae bond for $25,000, with a coupon of 6 percent. The next month, you would get a payment of $125 in interest—but you might also get a $75 payment of principal. Because you got a principal payment, you no longer have a full $25,000 that's earning interest in the bond; you have only $24,925. This return of principal might (or might not) continue with every payment, so that by the end of the year (depending on how quickly people are paying off their mortgages), you could have only $23,500 earning 6 percent. The next year, that amount could dwindle to $21,000, and so on. Your interest rate is staying the same, but the amount of money on which you are earning interest is declining.

People who invest in Ginnie Maes, Fannie Maes, and Freddie Macs tend to forget that these agencies are mortgage holders and that, as such, investors will be getting back some principal every month. Often, they spend the principal along with the interest, instead of reinvesting it. When the bond finally matures (or is paid back), these folks may have very little principal remaining in the bond, and that can be a rude shock.

Even so, U.S. mortgage–backed bonds are great bonds to look into, especially when interest rates are low and you would like a slightly higher interest rate. The minimum investment for an individual Ginnie Mae bond is $25,000; minimum investments in Fannie Maes and Freddie Macs vary according to the particular security, but tend to start lower. You also can invest in a Ginnie Mae fund, in which your minimum investment will be much lower. Make sure, however, that it is a no-load fund with low expense ratios.

CORPORATE BONDS

What are corporate bonds?

Corporate bonds (also called corporates) are debt obligations, or IOUs, issued by private and publicly traded corporations. They are typically issued in multiples of $1,000 or $5,000. Companies use the funds they raise from selling bonds for a variety of purposes, from building offices and factories and purchasing equipment to buying other companies.

When you buy a corporate bond, you are lending money to the corporation that issued it, which promises to return your money, or principal, at a specified maturity date. Until that time, the company also pays you a stated rate of interest, usually twice a year. The interest payments you receive from corporate bonds are taxable. Unlike stocks, bonds do not give you an ownership interest in the issuing corporation.

Is it easy to buy and sell corporate bonds?

Yes. The corporate bond market is large and liquid, with daily trading volume estimated at $10 billion. Bonds are bought and sold on two separate markets: the New York Stock Exchange (NYSE), where major corporations' debt issues are quoted and traded every day, and the over-the-counter (OTC) market, which is made up of bond dealers and brokers around the country. The OTC market is much bigger than the exchange market; most bond transactions, even those involving listed issues, take place in this market.

What are the benefits of investing in corporate bonds?

The benefits include yields that are usually higher than comparable-maturity government bonds or CDs; relative safety (based on credit rating); and marketability. If you must sell a bond before maturity, you can usually do so easily and quickly because of the size and liquidity of the market.

Who issues corporate bonds?

There are five main categories of issuers, representing various sectors of the economy. These include public utilities; transportation companies; industrial companies; financial services companies; and conglomerates. Issuers may be U.S. companies or foreign companies. Foreign governments are also frequent issuers in the U.S. market.

I've heard of a sinking-fund provision—what's that?

A sinking fund is money taken from a corporation's earnings that is used to redeem bonds periodically, before maturity. If a bond issue has a sinking-fund provision, a certain portion of the issue must be retired each year. It's like a call feature, except that the bonds retired are usually selected by lottery.

One investor benefit of a sinking fund is that it lowers the risk of default by reducing the amount of the corporation's outstanding debt over time. Another is that it provides price support for the bond in the secondary market, particularly in a period of rising interest rates. However, investors may also lose a source of income if their bond is called in. In a period of falling rates, they may have to reinvest their money at a lower rate.

What happens if the company whose bond I hold goes bankrupt?

If the company defaults on its debt or goes out of business, you, as a creditor, will have priority for repayment over stockholders. But you may not have priority over other creditors. The order of repayment depends on the specific terms of the bond, among other things. So-called "secured bonds" are usually the ones to look for if you want safety in case of a default.

What is a secured bond? And what does unsecured mean?

If a bond is secured, the issuer has pledged specific assets (known as collateral) that can be sold, if necessary, to pay the bondholders. If you buy a secured bond, you will "pay" for the extra safety in the form of a lower interest rate than you would have received on a comparable unsecured bond, which is simply an obligation to pay backed by the issuer's general credit, with no collateral pledged.

Give me a rundown of the different types of corporate bonds.

Sure. It goes like this:

- Debenture bonds. Most corporate bonds are debentures—that is, unsecured debt obligations repaid out of the corporation's earnings on its products or services. However, even unsecured bonds have additional security in the event that the company subsequently pledges its assets as collateral on other debt obligations.
- Mortgage bonds. These are bonds for which real estate or other physical property worth more than the bonds has been pledged as collateral. They are mostly issued by public utilities. Sometimes the same assets are also being pledged to a separate group of creditors, so whenever you invest in mortgage bonds, find out how much of the issuer's other debt is secured by the same collateral.
- Collateral trust bonds. A company can deposit stocks and other securities with a trustee as collateral for its bonds. The collateral must have a market value at least equal to the value of the bonds being secured.
- Equipment trust certificates. Typically, railroads and airlines issue these bonds as a way to pay for new equipment. A trustee holds the ownership of the equipment

until the loan is paid off, and the investors who buy the certificates usually have a first claim on the equipment.

- Subordinated debentures. Subordinated debentures are debt that is subordinated, or junior, and so has a lower repayment priority than that of other debt (but a higher priority than stocks). Only after secured bonds and debentures are paid off can holders of subordinated debentures be paid. In exchange for this lower level of security, investors earn a higher rate of interest.

- Guaranteed bonds. Guaranteed bonds are actually guaranteed by another corporation—that is, a corporation different from the one that issued the debt. For example, bonds issued by an incorporated subsidiary of a company might be guaranteed by its parent corporation.

How do I pay taxes on corporate bonds?

Interest payments from corporate bonds are subject to federal and state income taxes at your ordinary income tax rate. (If you own shares in bond mutual funds, your interest will come to you in the form of "dividends," but these are fully taxable, too.)

What is the minimum investment in a corporate bond?

Bonds are issued and sold in $1,000 denominations. For OTC bonds, the minimum investment is usually $5,000.

How much is the commission on a corporate bond?

Brokers often sell bonds from their firms' inventory, in which case investors do not pay an outright commission. Rather, they pay a markup that is built into the price quoted for the bond. If a broker has to go out into the market to find a particular bond for a customer, a commission may be charged. Each firm establishes its own markups and commissions, which may vary depending on the size of the transaction and the type of bond you are buying. Please shop around.

CONVERTIBLE BONDS

I've heard that you can buy bonds that can later be converted to stocks. Is that right?
Yes, it is. Convertible bonds are issued by corporations as debt with the option to convert the bond into stock, or ownership, in that company at a predetermined price.

How do I know if convertible bonds are right for me?
If you want the possibility of some growth in the value of your investment along with income, convertible bonds are well worth looking into. But be aware that when you buy a convertible bond, you may trade some income for growth, so these may not be for you if pure income is your goal. Also, the conversion feature and the quality of the corporation issuing the bonds is key here. Make sure that you understand these features before investing. These bonds tend to be far less liquid than others, so, again, be careful.

HIGH-YIELD ("JUNK") BONDS

What are high-yield bonds, and why are they called "junk" bonds?
A high-yield bond is simply any bond rated below BBB by a major rating agency, meaning that it is not "investment grade." Such bonds are typically issued by young companies without much of a credit history, by foreign companies, and by larger, older companies in some degree of trouble. Their rating—perhaps unfairly called a "junk" rating—reflects a negative view

of the bond issuer's creditworthiness. The weaker a company's financial condition, the higher the interest rate it must pay to borrow money. Hence these bonds are called "high-yield" or "junk."

Are all junk bonds dangerous?

Some are more dangerous than others. Quality differences among junk bond issues are huge. To be on the safer side, look for bonds rated BB and Ba or higher.

Do high-yield bonds trade just like other bonds?

High-yield bonds often trade more like stocks than like high-quality bonds such as Treasuries. They can be dangerous in recessions. Whereas high-quality bonds usually provide strong returns during recessions because their prices rise as interest rates fall, high-yield bonds, like stocks, may decline as company earnings (so important for repayment) fall off. In a recovery, high-yield bonds can outperform high-quality bonds, because the rise in corporate earnings is more important than the threat of rising interest rates—at least for a while.

Can you give me an idea of what the total return on high-yield bonds has been over the past few years?

Yes. Total return of junk bonds for each of the 15 years through 2005, based on the Credit Suisse High-Yield Index, are as follows:

YEAR	TOTAL RETURN
1990	-6.4%
1991	43.8%
1992	16.7%
1993	18.9%
1994	-1.0%

1995	17.4%
1996	12.4%
1997	12.6%
1998	0.6%
1999	3.3%
2000	-5.21%
2001	5.80%
2002	3.10%
2003	27.94%
2004	11.95%
2005	2.26%

Source: Credit Suisse

If I do not have much money to invest, is it better to buy individual junk bonds or a junk-bond fund?

As you will see in the Buyer Beware section later in this chapter, I am not a great fan of bond funds. As for individual high-yield bonds, they are not for the conservative investor, especially one with a small amount of money.

What should I keep in mind when investing in high-yield bonds?

Just remember the old saying, "There is no such thing as a free lunch." Junk bonds are not easy money. The price of receiving above-average income is above-average risk—the risk of potential price declines if you try to sell your bond on the secondary market. That market is not as active—as liquid—as the market for stocks or high-grade bonds, and even though returns on high-yield bonds have historically rewarded the investor for the additional risk, there is no guarantee that this will be true in the future.

ZERO COUPON BONDS

What is a zero coupon bond?

A "zero coupon bond," also known as a strip, is a bond that can be issued by a corporation, government, or government agency. Like other bonds, it has a coupon, or interest rate, of a certain percentage. However, unlike most other bonds (but like EE/E bonds and Treasury bills), the income that a zero coupon generates is not paid out to you; it stays in the bond, earning interest at the original rate. This can be a great advantage in a high-interest-rate environment.

Is there anything I should be careful of with zero coupon bonds?

Yes. One characteristic of a zero coupon bond is that, even though your interest is reinvested rather than paid out to you, you are expected to pay income taxes on that money. To get around this, you can purchase zero coupon bonds in your IRA, or else buy a municipal zero coupon bond that is federally tax-free. Also, the market value of these bonds tends to be more volatile than that of conventional bonds with respect to price movements and interest rates. Be careful if you think that interest rates are heading up and you think you might have to sell your bond before its maturity date—you could take quite a hit when you sell.

How much do I pay for a zero coupon bond?

When you buy a zero coupon bond, you ordinarily do so at a discount. For example, if in the year 2000 you bought a zero coupon bond with a face value of $50,000 maturing in the year 2008 with a coupon of 5 percent, it might cost you around $30,500 up front. When the bond matures, if you haven't sold it, you would get $50,000 back.

Is there only one kind of zero coupon bond, or are there several?

Zero coupon bonds come in many variations—such as zero coupon Treasuries, municipals, and occasionally corporates. Regardless of the issuer, it is essential that you get one with insurance. Since the interest is not being paid to you, nothing could be worse than if the bond defaulted and you got nothing at all from it, not even the interest income.

What would you say is the best thing about zero coupon bonds?

The upside of zero coupon bonds is that in a high-interest-rate environment when rates are expected to come down, zero coupon bonds let you reinvest your interest at your original higher rate. In fact, any decline in the rate environment could make this investment well worth your while, since the price of zero coupon bonds tends to go up in response to falling rates faster than that of conventional bonds. But the opposite is also true—when interest rates go up, zero coupons decrease in market value more rapidly than conventional bonds. This type of bond is volatile.

Still, zero coupon bonds are very useful for keeping the money in your retirement account safe, sound, and growing. Or consider this scenario: You may know without a doubt how much money you are going to need by a certain date, for example, to pay for college. Very few investments other than certain Treasuries and a zero coupon bond can assure you of a certain return on a certain date. That is because no other investment can lock in the rate of return for the reinvestment of your interest.

ADDITIONAL RESOURCES

PICKING AND CHOOSING STOCKS
ON THE INTERNET

www.morningstar.com This site lists company information and easy-to-understand stock data and analysis, as well as general stock and bond investing educational articles.

www.hoovers.com A comprehensive resource with free and premium company information.

www.investors.com *Investors Business Daily*'s website offers a wealth of information.

www.suzeorman.com Or visit my website with its extensive resource center.

DISCOUNT BROKERS

TD Ameritrade
www.tdameritrade.com
(800) 934-4448
Offers a wide range of products and services.

Muriel Siebert
www.siebertnet.com
(800) 872-0444
No account fees, and this website includes many research tools.

E* Trade Financial
www.etrade.com
(800) 387-2331
Many experienced investors swear by E* Trade.

FINANCIAL MAGAZINES, NEWSPAPERS, AND ADVICE

The Wall Street Journal
www.wsj.com
(800) 369-2834
The dean of business dailies.

Barron's
www.barrons.com
(800) 369-2834
One of several can't-do-without financial bibles for investors, large and small.

Bob Brinker
www.bobbrinker.com
One of my favorite financial newsletters.

Investor's Business Daily
www.investors.com
(800) 831-2525
This classic publication contains informative data and articles about investing.

Smart Money magazine
www.smartmoney.com
Terrific, timely stock and bond coverage as well as useful tutorials.

Money magazine
www.money.cnn.com
The website's Money 101 section offers easy-to-understand lessons in all aspects of investing.

The American Association of Individual Investors (AAII)
P.O. Box 11092
Chicago, IL 60611-9737
www.aaii.com
A critical resource for beginning investors.

QUESTIONS ABOUT SECURITIES OR BROKERAGES

Securities Investor Protection Corporation (SIPC)
www.sipc.org

National Association of Security Dealers
www.nasd.org
(800) 289-9999

Securities and Exchange Commission
www.sec.gov
(202) 942-8088

BOND-RATING SERVICES AND INFORMATION

Standard & Poor's
www.standardandpoors.com
(202) 438-2400

Moody's
www.moodys.com
(212) 553-0377

A.M. Best
www.ambest.com
(908) 439-2200

Duff & Phelps
www.fitchratings.com
(312) 263-2610

TreasuryDirect
(800) 943-6864
www.treasurydirect.gov

Index

INDEX

ABOUT SUZE ORMAN

SUZE ORMAN has been called "a force in the world of personal finance" and a "one-woman financial advice powerhouse" by *USA Today*. A two-time Emmy® Award–winning television show host, *New York Times* best-selling author, magazine and online columnist, writer-producer, and motivational speaker, Suze is undeniably America's most recognized personal finance expert.

Suze has written five consecutive *New York Times* best sellers—*The Money Book for the Young, Fabulous & Broke*; *The Laws of Money, The Lessons of Life*; *The Road to Wealth, The Courage to Be Rich*; and *The 9 Steps to Financial Freedom*—as well as the national best sellers *Suze Orman's Financial Guidebook* and *You've Earned It, Don't Lose It*. Her most recent book, *Women & Money*, was published by Spiegel & Grau in February 2007. A newspaper column, also called "Women & Money," syndicated by Universal Press Syndicate, began in January 2007. Additionally, she has created *Suze Orman's FICO*

Kit, Suze Orman's Will & Trust Kit, Suze Orman's Insurance Kit, The Ask Suze Library System, and *Suze Orman's Ultimate Protection Portfolio.*

Suze has written, coproduced, and hosted five PBS specials based on her *New York Times* best-selling books. She is the single most successful fund-raiser in the history of public television, and recently won her second Daytime Emmy® Award in the category of Outstanding Service Show Host. Suze won her first Emmy® in 2004, in the same category.

Suze is contributing editor to *O, The Oprah Magazine* and *O at Home* and has a biweekly column, "Money Matters," on Yahoo! Finance. Suze hosts her own award-winning national CNBC-TV show, *The Suze Orman Show,* which airs every Saturday night, as well as *Financial Freedom Hour* on QVC television.

Suze has been honored with three American Women in Radio and Television (AWRT) Gracie Allen Awards. This award recognizes the nation's best radio, television, and cable programming for, by, and about women. In 2003, Suze garnered her first Gracie for *The Suze Orman Show* in the National/Network/Sydication Talk show category. She won her second and third Gracies in the Individual Achievement: Program Host category in 2005 and 2006.

Profiled in *Worth* magazine's 100th issue as among those "who have revolutionized the way America thinks about money," Suze also was named one of *Smart Money* magazine's top thirty "Power Brokers," defined as those who have most influenced the mutual fund industry and affected our money, in 1999. A 2003 inductee into the Books for a Better Life (BBL) Award Hall of Fame in recognition of her ongoing contributions to self-improvement, Suze previously received the 1999 BBL Motivational Book Award for *The Courage to Be Rich.* As a tribute to her continuing involvement, in 2002 the organization established the Suze Orman First Book Award to honor a first-time author of a self-improvement book in any category. She received a 2003 Crossing Borders Award from the Feminist Press. The award recognizes a distinguished group of women who not only have excelled in remarkable careers but also have shown great courage, vision, and conviction by forging new places for women in their respective fields. In 2002, Suze was selected as one of five distinguished recipients of the prestigious TJFR Group News Luminaries Award, which honors lifetime achievement in business journalism.

A sought-after motivational speaker, Suze has lectured widely throughout the United States, South Africa, and Asia to audiences of up to fifty thousand people, and often appearing alongside individuals such as Colin Powell, Rudy Giuliani, Jerry Lewis, Steve Forbes, and Donald Trump. She has been featured in almost every major publication in the United States and has appeared numerous times on *The View*, *Larry King Live*, and *The Oprah Winfrey Show*.

A Certified Financial Planner®, Suze directed the Suze Orman Financial Group from 1987 to 1997, served as vice president of investments for Prudential Bache Securities from 1983 to 1987, and from 1980 to 1983 was an account executive at Merrill Lynch. Prior to that, she worked as a waitress at the Buttercup Bakery in Berkeley, California, from 1973 to 1980.